THE POLYPHONIC SEQUENCES IN CODEX WOLFENBUETTEL 677

by

Bryan R. Gillingham

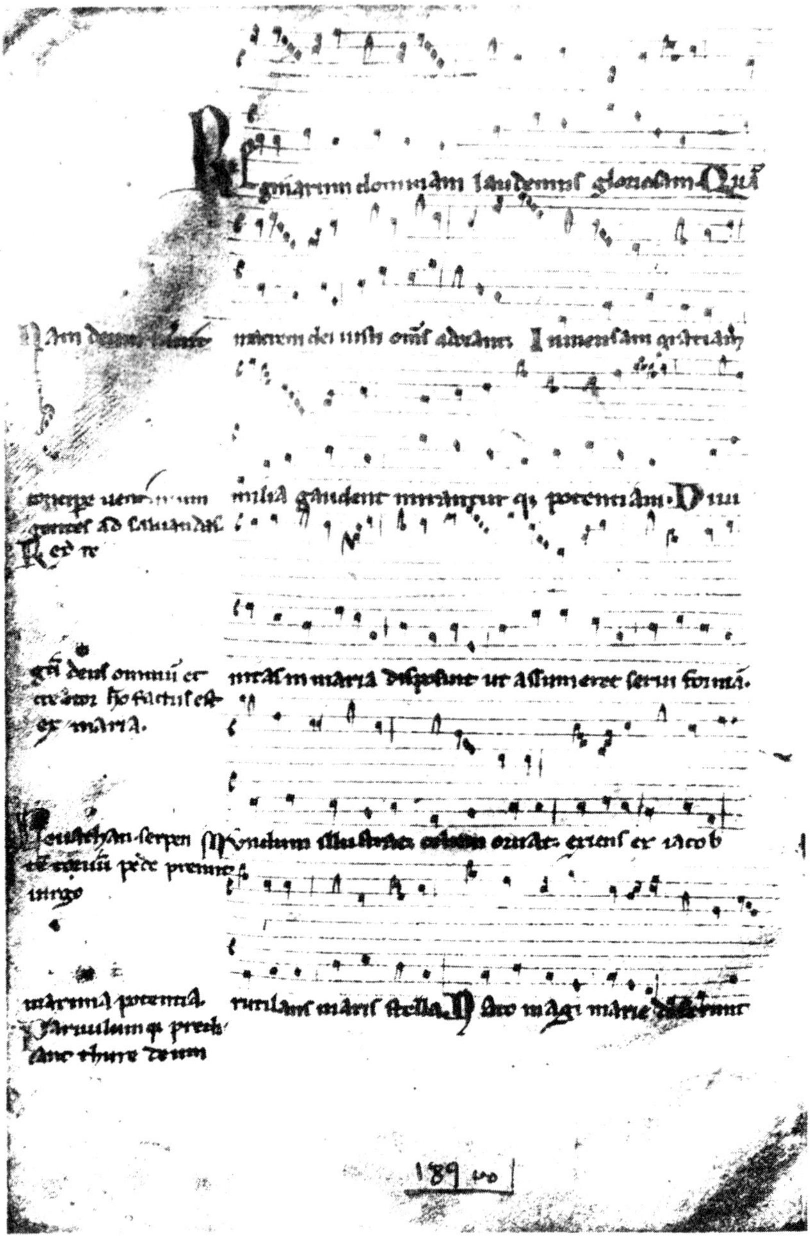

Frontispiece
A facsimile of a part of the sequence
Reginarum dominam, W_1, f. 189_v.

Wissenschaftliche Abhandlungen
Band XXXV

Musicological Studies
Vol. XXXV

The Polyphonic Sequences in Codex Wolfenbuettel 677

by

Bryan Gillingham

The Institute of Mediaeval Music, Ltd.
L'Institut de Musique Médiévale, S. A.
Das Institut für Mittelalterliche Musikforschung, GmbH.

Henryville—Ottawa—Binningen

Institute of Mediaeval Music, Ltd.
Post Office Box 295
Henryville, Pa. USA-18332

Institut de Musique Médiévale, S. A.
Case postale 6439, Succursale «J»
Ottawa (Ont.) K2A 3Y5

Institut für Mittelalterliche Musikforschung, GmbH
Melchtalstraße 11
CH-4102 Binningen

Standard internationale Numerierung der Bücher Nr. 931902-14-2
Imprimé aux Etats-Unis par Sun Litho, Stroudsburg, Pennsylvanie.

To Terence Bailey,

for constant inspiration, encouragement, and support.

CONTENTS

LIST OF TRANSCRIPTIONS

ABBREVIATIONS

Analecta Hymnica	G. M. Dreves, in collaboration with C. Blume and H. Bannister. *Analecta Hymnica.* 55 vols. Leipzig: O. R. Reisland, 1886-1922.
Kehrein	Josef Kehrein. *Lateinische Sequenzen des Mittelalters.* Mainz: F. Kupferberg, 1873.
Milchsack	Gustav Milchsack. *Hymni et Sequentiae cum pluribus aliis et Latinis et Gallicis necnon Theotuscis Carminibus medio aevo compositis.* Halle a/S: Maximiliani Niemeyer, 1886.
RISM	*Répertoire International des Sources Musicales.* (A continuing series, with various editors and publishers, sponsored by the International Musicological Society and the International Association of Music Libraries.)

PREFACE

One of the central problems of music of the twelfth and thirteenth centuries is that of rhythm. Prior to the advent of modal rhythm, it is unclear whether meter was quantitative, equal, or accentual, despite adamant claims by scholars for each of these. One question that perhaps has not been asked enough is, where did notated modal rhythm come from? Was it a cataclysmic invention of Leonin? Or a return to the metrical theories of St. Augustine? Or did it spring from some other source? The answer to this and related questions is not to be found through purely literary or musical study, but by a combination of the two. Nor is the answer provided adequately from theoretical speculations. As with so many "innovations" in the arts, novel developments are often not so revolutionary as they first seem to be, but proceed from practical experimentation.

What follows is an examination and edition of a small group of sequences, done in as complete a manner as possible, with attention to poetic and musical elements, as well as theoretical speculations. It is hoped that the results might be of some benefit to musicologists and philologists. The present writer would like to thank the University of Western Ontario for allowing some material from a recent article in Studies in Music to be reproduced here.

B. G.

INTRODUCTION

By the late twelfth century, when Leonin and Perotin were active, the setting of polyphonic sequences had become an established tradition. Sequentors had been setting polyphonic sequences since the middle of the ninth century at least, and monophonic sequences may well have been a basis for improvised organum long before that. Polyphonic sequences survive in well-known treatises dating from the ninth to the eleventh century, and appear in manuscripts such as the Winchester Tropers, Codex Calixtinus, as well as several collections from St. Martial.[1] In addition to evanescent features encountered generally in organum from the ninth to the twelfth century, the polyphonic sequence during the same period reflected stylistic changes inherent in its monophonic counterpart, especially since the latter generally functioned as the tenor (or *vox principalis)* for the former.

On the basis of both poetry and music, four main types (or phases) of monophonic sequences can be isolated to about the time of Perotin's death. The first of these, represented in sequences of the ninth and tenth century by Notker, and others to be found in the repertories of St. Martial, Winchester, and elsewhere, has been called misleadingly, the "classical" or "standardized" sequence. The classical sequence, however, lacks the balance which would normally be associated with its epithet; it is characterized by sprawling, unequal versicles, absence of poetic rhyme and symbolism, a-parallelism in first and last versicles, and a fairly close association with the Alleluia. It might better be referred to as "irregular." During its next phase in the eleventh century, a transitional phase represented well by Wipo's *Victimae paschali,* the sequence began a process of levelling or balancing, in which it became more symmetrical in terms of versicle lengths, began to indulge in poetic rhyme (albeit inconsistent), and made some use of symbolism. By the twelfth century, the sequence had become truly "classical" in that it had achieved pervasive symmetry in versicle length, consistent usage of double and interlocking rhyme, had begun to bristle with poetic symbols, had abandoned initial and terminal single versicles to a large extent, and adopted recurring 8/8/7 (8/7 or 8/8/8/7) syllabification for half versicles. The designation "regular" is aptly suited to such sequences, many of which have been attributed to Adam of St. Victor. After Adam, in the late twelfth and early thirteenth centuries, various new

1 For a detailed discussion of the development of sequences from the ninth to eleventh centuries, see Bryan Gillingham, "A History of the Polyphonic Sequence in the Middle Ages" (Ph. D. dissertation, University of Washington, 1976), pp. 1-138.

syllabification schemes (etc., 6/6/6, 7/7/7, 7/7/6, etc.) were introduced but used in the same consistent manner as they were in the regular sequence; these latest efforts may collectively be referred to as "mature" sequences. It should be added that certain characteristics typified the sequence through all four phases; these are, a preference for syllabic setting, musical rhyme at the ends of successive versicles, modal preference (Dorian and Mixolydian prevailing), and the extensive use of cadences which can be referred to as "sequence cadences" (i. e., cadences of the following type:

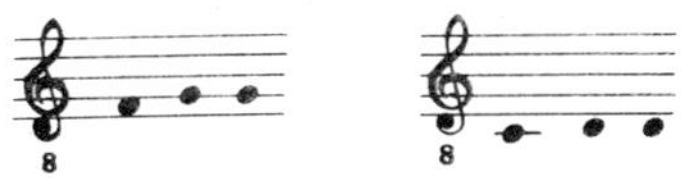

The polyphonic sequence, while reflecting the various changes in the monophonic sequence mentioned above, was a progressive genre which aptly demonstrated general trends in the development of early polyphony. Following its probable first function as a *vox principalis* for improvised parallel organum, simple and composite, at the fourth, fifth, and octave, the sequence, as illustrated in *Musica Enchiriadis* and elsewhere, [2] was employed as an upper principal voice in converging organum which featured oblique motion mixed with a predominance of parallel fourths. Strict note-against-note writing typified the sequence until the turn of the millenium when occasional groups of two and three notes in the organal voice were set against single notes in the principal voice; such incidents may be observed in sequences from the Winchester Tropers. During the eleventh century, the incidence of neumatic and or melismatic groups in the added voice increased, and the *vox principalis* (or tenor) reversed its position and became the lower voice, as may be observed in some Compostela and St. Martial examples. By the time the Notre Dame school had taken pre-eminence in the development of polyphony, after further experimentation in independent part writing and an increase in the use of contrary motion in the early twelfth century, the polyphonic sequence had adopted a style midway between conductus and sustained-tone organal style.

After the polyphonic sequence had passed through a period of experimentation at the hands of St. Martial and Compostela musicians, and had subsequently attained a degree of stability, ironically, the compilers of the four so-called Notre Dame manuscripts [3] (judging from the

2 *Ibidem,* pp. 86-106.

3 Although much transcriptional work remains to be done, all four are

material which has survived) began to neglect the sequence in favour of genres which better lent themselves to polyphony, such as conductus, clausula, organum, and motet. It is no surprise that the sequence, having a relatively lengthy text, should yield to music with shorter or strophically repeated texts, for the sheer work involved in setting up to thirteen (or more) through-composed stanzas to two, three, or four voices, particularly if melisma was to be a feature, must have been daunting. Whereas a few two-voiced sequences managed to win a place in these codices, there is none for three or four voices. [4]

The most important assemblage of polyphonic sequences in the Notre Dame collections resides in the oldest fascicle of Codex Wolfenbüttel 677 (W_1), or the St. Andrews manuscript, [5] and the bulk of the following discussion will focus on them. But first the contents of the other three manuscripts should be surveyed. W_1 the earliest of the four manuscripts in terms of compositional date, is succeeded by F, the music of which was composed about 1200. [6] It contains no collection of sequences such as W_1, nor are there any individual ones, in spite of the existence of many conducti which textually resemble sequences. The situation does not improve with the next manuscript, Ma. [7] However, W_2, the latest of the Notre Dame codices, includes a two-voiced setting of the very popular sequence *Verbum bonum et suave.* [8]

available in facsimile, as follows: J. H. Baxter, editor, *An Old St. Andrews Music Book* (London: Oxford University Press, 1931); Luther Dittmer, editor, *Firenze Biblioteca Mediceo-Laurenziana, Pluteo 29,1* (Brooklyn, N. Y.: The Institute of Mediaeval Music, Publications of Mediaeval Musical Manuscripts Nos. 10 and 11, 1968 and 1971); Dittmer, editor, *Madrid 20846* (Brooklyn, N. Y.:The Institute of Mediaeval Music, Publications of Mediaeval Musical Manuscripts No. 1, 1958); and Dittmer, editor, *Wolfenbuttel 1099* (Brooklyn, N. Y.: The Institute of Mediaeval Music, Publications of Mediaeval Musical Manuscripts No. 2, 1960). These will be abbreviated W_1, F, Ma, and W_2 respectively.

4 For confirmation, see the above facsimiles and Heinrich Husmann, *Die drei- und vierstimmigen Notre Dame- Organa* (Hildesheim: Georg Olms, 1967).

5 Described in Friedrich Ludwig, *Repertorium Organorum Recentioris et Motetorum Vetustissimi Stili* (Brooklyn, N. Y.: The Institute of Mediaeval Music, 1964), I,1, 7-10.

6 *Ibidem,* p. 57.

7 *Ibidem,* 125 ff.

8 G. A. Anderson, *The Latin Compositions in Fascicules VII and VIII of the Notre Dame Manuscript Wolfenbu*ttel 1099 (1206) (Brooklyn, N. Y.: The Institute of Mediaeval Music, 1968), p. 82, calls it an *unicum.* It would be better called an elaboration or variant (a common occurrence with sequences), even though it is not identical in the upper voice to other medieval versions.

It is curious, and perhaps significant, that *Verbum bonum et suave* should be grouped together in W_2 with eight other two-voiced conducti.[9] Ludwig recognizes that the work is a sequence although he classifies it as a conductus;[10] Anderson admits that it is a sequence but prefers to call it a conductus.[11] Admittedly, it is a short sequence, similar in style to the conducti which surround it, but most of them are sequence-influenced. One of them derives its text from the fifth versicle of the sequence *Laetabundus;*[12] and *Si deus est animas* relates to a stanza of the sequence *Epiphaniam Domino:*[13] another, *Crucifigat omnes,* has structural links with the estampie,[14] having been called by Ellinwood a "strophic sequence."[15] The relationship between sequence and conductus is not restricted to the small group of conducti in W_2.[16] One is struck by the numerous conducti in the Notre Dame manuscripts (and many others) which display elements of textual imagery, meter, versification, and musical structuring which resemble those of the sequence; in other words, they often seem to be textual and/or musical compressions of the more linearly expansive sequences. Many other examples of sequence-based conducti could be offered here, but that could lead us astray; suffice it to say that the sequence preceded the conductus as a preferred genre (thousands were written before the heyday of the conductus), and that the conductus drew heavily on its predecessor and partially ousted it as polyphony developed.

The sequence was probably performed by a divided choir, split group of soloists, or soloist(s) and choir, with one group following the other, and because of its manner of performance, its enormous popularity, the impracticality of setting it polyphonically, and its priority in time compared to the conductus, the meaning of the latter, as a participial substantive of the third conjugation verb *conducere* ("to bring together" or "unite") would have been perfectly appropriate. The

9 W_2, ff. 138v-144v.

10 Ludwig, *opere citato,* pp. 180-181.

11 Anderson, *opere citato,* p. 64.

12 *Yzaias cecinit,* W_2, f. 141,

13 Anderson, *opere citato,* p. 87. For further examples of sequence elements in conducti, see idem, "Thirteenth-Century Conductus: Obiter dicta," *The Musical Quarterly,* LVIII (1972), 349-364; and idem, "Symbolism in Texts of Thirteenth-Century Music," *Studies in Music,* IV (1970), 19-59.

14 Anderson, *The Latin Compositions...,* p. 64.

15 Leonard Ellinwood, "The Conductus," *The Musical Quarterly,* XXVII (1941), 175.

16 For more examples, see *ibidem,* p. 175.

generally accepted definition of the conductus differs from that given above, and is, in Ellinwood's words, "a Latin metrical poem set in music in from one to four parts during the twelfth and thirteenth centuries, used for festive or processional purposes both within and without the church." [17] The emphasis on the "processional purposes" *(conducere* can also mean "to lead" or "to escort") have perhaps been overplayed, for Ellinwood admits that only Johannes de Grocheo described it in such terms. [18] A conductus, therefore, would more likely have been conceived as a work compressed into note-against-note or discant style, performed by a "united" choir, without alternatim between two groups as in the sequence, and hence would lend itself more readily to the vertical expansion that characterized developing polyphony.

Of more immediate concern is the eleventh fascicle of W_1, likely the oldest fascicle (notationally, stylistically, and in manuscript and compositional date) in all the four Notre Dame sources, even though its date has not been conclusively established yet. Estimates of its date range from the early twelfth century to the fourteenth, but the most convincing of these places its compositional date at about 1170 or slightly earlier. [19] Positioned last in W_1, its content differs considerably from that of the other fascicles in the codex, and in studying it some years ago, Handschin suggested that it had its origin in England rather than France. [20] Although his hypothesis might have some validity in application to the polyphonic style, it fails to convince when applied to both the sequence texts and the tenor melodies, most of which were well-known, or composed, on the Continent. [21] All the pieces in the eleventh fascicle differ generally from most Notre Dame compositons in that they cannot be classed as conducti, organa, clausulae, or motets (with some exceptions), but this can be attributed as much to early date as to provenance. The works making up the fascicle include seven Kyrie tropes, one Gloria trope, nine Alleluias and one Tract, fourteen sequences, [22] one hymn, eight offertories and antiphons, four Sanctus

17 *Ibidem,* p. 175.

18 *Ibidem,* p. 167.

19 For more on this, see E. H. Sanders, "Peripheral Polyphony of the Thirteenth Century," *The Journal of the American Musicological Society,* XVII (1964), 261-263; Yvonne Rokseth, *Polyphonies du XIII_e Siècle* (Paris: l'Oiseau Lyre, 1939), IV, 40-41; Rudolf Flotzinger, *Der Discantussatz im Magnus Liber und seine Nachfolge* (Wien: Hermann Bohlaus Nachf., 1969), 232 ff,; W_1, v-xiii; Ludwig, *opere citato,* pp., 7-10; and Edward H. Roesner, "The Origins of W_1," *The Journal of the American Musicological Society,* XXIX (1976), 337-380.

20 Jacques Handschin, "A Monument of English Mediaeval Polyphony," *The Musical Times,* LXXIII (1932), 511; and LXXIV (1933), 698.

21 Sanders, *opere citato,* p. 261, also objects to the hypothesis.

22 Ludwig, *opere citato,* p. 9; and RISM, Ser. B, IV/1, 98, include *Ave Maria*

tropes, and three Agnus tropes.[23] All the piec are for two voices in a style midway between that of the conductus a.,d Leonin organum.

To the present writer's knowledge, few of the fourteen sequences have been edited, and those that have are open to question.[24] No thorough editorial study, supported by transcriptions, has been done on the whole group, and hence the remainder of this study will be given over to such a task, and, in particular, to the crucial matter of rhythm. The practical results of the theories presented here may be assessed in the transcriptions at the end. As will be shown, these fourteen sequences represent a stage in which musical notation in most ways was not a significant indicator of rhythm: in other words, a stage of transition between two different notational systems. The invaluable information inherent in them can be progressively and retrospectively extrapolated. Unlike their monophonic counterparts, the W_1 sequences include the additional informative parameter of a second voice, without which, the assessment of rhythm, prior to modal notation (as opposed to modal imposition), is largely guesswork.

Before any meaningful analysis of the fourteen sequences at issue can be undertaken, the method of transcription must be explained and justified. The realization of pitches presents few difficulties, but the ambiguously-notated rhythm is quite another matter, and as a preparation for the empirical discussions which follow (and for a general analysis), a number of theorists have been consulted. Their thoughts were recorded variously before, during, and after compilation of the sequences in question; the excerpts from their writings pertain to rhythm, sequences, and poetry in general, but not always to all three. First the writers speak for themselves, then afterwards their remarks are summarized and evaluated:[25]

gratia plena (f. 192-192v) in the sequence group, but musically, it is not structured in progressively repeated parallel versicles like the others; we suggest, therefore, that it is a strophic two-voiced prayer to the Virgin with similarities to the hymn and conductus. Thus, there are fourteen, rather than fifteen sequences.

23 For more details, see the preface of W_1; Ludwig, *opere citato,* pp. 7-11; and RISM, Ser. B, IV/1, pp. 97-171.

24 For transcriptions with which the present writer disagrees, see Ellinwood, *opere citato,* p. 189; Handschin, "A Monument....," LXXIV, 698; Ian Bent, "A New Polyphonic Verbum bonum et suave," *Music and Letters,* LI (1970), 238; and Flotzinger, *opere citato,* Anhang 18.

25 The translations are by the present writer unless otherwise specified in footnotes.

1. St. Augustine (from De Musica Libri Sex, ca. 388 A. D.) [26]

> Sane arbitror jam te intelligere innumerabilia genera esse metrorum, quae quingenta sexaginta octo inveneramus, cum et de silentiis non nisi finalibus exempla essent data, et nulla pedum commixtio facta esset, et nulla solutio longarum in duas breves, quae pedem ultra syllabas quatuor porriget. At si adhibita omni silentorium interpositione, et omni pedum commixtione, et omni solutione longarum colligere numerum metrorum velis; tantus existit, ut nomen ejus fortasse non suppetat.

(I think you now certainly understand there are a great many kinds of meter. In fact, we found there were 568 when no examples were given of rests except final ones, and no resolution of long syllables into two shorts stretching the foot to more than four syllables. But if you wish to get the number of meters with every possible insertion of rests applied, and every combination of feet, and every resolution of long syllables, the number is so great its name perhaps is not at hand.)

2. Isidore of Seville (from the Etymologiarum, ca. 600) [27]

> Pedes sunt qui certis syllabarum temporibus insistunt, nec a legitimo spatio unquam recedunt. Pedes dicti, eo quod per ipsos metra ambulent. Nam sicut nos pedibus incedimus, ita metra quasi pedibus pradiuntur. Pedes autem omnes centum viginti quatuor sunt; disyllabi quatuor, trisyllabi octo, tetrasyllabi sexdecim, pentasyllabi duo et triginta, hexasyllabi quatuor et sexaginta.

(Feet are those things which depend on the fixed times of syllables, nor do they ever depart from their correct space. Feet are so called because meters walk through them. For just as we march on our feet, so meters walk as if on feet. The total number of feet is 124: four disyllables, eight trisyllables, sixteen tetrasyllables, thirty-two pentasyllables, and sixty-four hexasyllables.)

26 *OEuvres de Saint Augustin,* ed. Finnaert et Thonnard (Paris, Desclée, De Brouwer, et Cie, 1936), VII, 286; translation by R. C. Taliaferro, *St. Augustine on Music* (Annapolis: The St. John's Bookstore, 1939), p. 120.

27 J. P. Migne, *Patrologiae Cursus Completus. Series Latina* (Turnholti,Belgium: Typographi Brepos Editores Pontificii, 1844-1864), LXXXII, col. 90.

3. Guido of Arezzo (from Expositiones in Micrologum, eleventh century) [28]

> Metricos autem dico cantus, quia saepe ita canimus, ut quasi versus pedibus scandere videamur, sicut fit, cum ipsa metra canimus in quibus cavendum est, ne superfluae continuentur neumae dissyllabae, sine admixtione trisyllabarum atquae tetrasyllabarum. Sicut enim lyrici poetae nunc hos nunc alios iunxere pedes, ita et qui cantum faciunt, rationabiliter diversas ac discretas neumas componant.

(I mention chants [the author has just referred to prosers and sequentiaries,] because we often sing in such a way that we seem to scan verses in feet, as is done when we sing the very meters in which care must be taken, lest they contain superfluous disyllabic neumes, without a mingling of trisyllables and tetrasyllables. Just as lyric poets join now these feet, now those, so those who make chant must arrange the diverse and discrete neumes rationally.)

4. Matthieu de Vendôme (from *Ars Versificatoria,* ca. 1175) [29]

> Amplius, materia de qua aliquis agere proponet, aut erit illibata, aut ab aliquo poeta primitus exsecuta. Si exsecuta fuerit, juxta tenorem poeticae narrationis erit procedendum, tali quidem consideratione, ut quaedam collateralia quae non sunt de principali propositio, scilicet comparationes et poeticae abusiones et figurativae constructiones, modus temporum et syllabarum, non inducantur.
>
> . . . . .

28 J. Smits van Waesberghe, *Expositiones in Micrologum Guidonis Aretini* (Amsterdam, 1957), p. 85.

29 E. Faral, *Les Arts Poètiques du XII$_e$ et du XIII$_e$ Siècle* (Paris: Librairie Ancienne Honoré Champion, 1924), p. 180.

> Antiquis siquidem incumbebat materiam protelare quibusdam diversiculis et collateralibus sententiis, ut materiae penuria poetico figmento plenius exuberans in artificiosum luxuriaret incrementum. Hoc autem modernis non licet. Vetera enim cessavere novis supervenientibus. Amplius, poeticas abusiones in syllabarum temporibus non debemus imitari. Non enim veritas sive analogia ab his expresse exigenda est, quibus erat pro ratione voluntas: nobis siquidem cederet ad culpam quod eis aspirabat ad indulgentiam. Nulla siquidem modernis permittitur in temporibus syllabarum transgressio, nisi duae, scilicet pentymemeris et synolimpha: pentymemeris id est semiquinaria diviso minoribus, synolimpha provectioribus omnibus.

(Furthermore, the material from which someone proposes to do this [i. e., to write a poem] will either be freely created or accomplished first by some other poet. If it is modelled on a previous poem, it must be carried out in like manner to the poet's narration, in such consideration of it, that the addition of those things which are not from the original subject, that is to say, the comparisons, the poetic usages, the figurative constructions, and the manner [*modus*] of times [*temporum*], are not eradicated.

. . . . .

It was incumbent upon the ancients to yoke material in some diversified and connected sentences, in order that penury of material fully overflowing in poetic invention might luxuriate into artificial offspring. However, this is not allowed by the moderns. Indeed, the old masters have been left idle by the new developments. Moreover, we must not imitate their poetic usages in the times of the syllables. The reality or proportion, in which there was an inclination towards reason, certainly must not be expelled from these; but for us it might yield to a fault which for them approached indulgence. In no way is a transgression in the times of syllables permitted by the moderns, except for two instances, that is to say, pentymemeris and synolimpha; pentymemeris is a semiquinarian division in minors, and synolimpha in which everything has been prolonged.) [30]

30 Charles Anthon, *A System of Latin Prosody and Metre* (New York: Harper and Bros., 1860), p. 102, describes pentymemeris as a division of five shorts or half-parts making up two and one-half feet. Synolimpha (synoloepha?) is perhaps a merging of syllables or ellision.

5. Geoffrey of Vinsauf (from *Poetria Nova,* ca. 1208-1214) [31]

Legibus arctetur metrum, sed prosa vagatur
Liberiore via, quia prosae publica strata
Admittit passim redas et plaustra; sed arta
Semita versiculi non vult tam grossa, sed ipsas
Voces in forma gracili, ne corpus agreste
Verbi mole sua perturbet et inquinet illum
Vultque venire metrum tanquam domicellula, compto
Crine, nitente gena, subtili corpore, forma
Egregia. Seriem tantae dulcedinis auri
Nescit habere parem jocunda decentia metri.
Prosaicus versus res grossior: omnia verba
Indistanter amat... .
Cetera non variat ratio, sed, carmine metri
Legibus astricto vel ab ejus lege soluto,
Ars eadem semper, quamvis quod pendet ab arte
Non sit semper idem. Sic verba domentur utrimque:
Arida non veniant, sed eis sententia succum,
Imprimat, et succo veniant et sanguine plena,
Nei quicquam puerile sonent... .

(Metrical composition is confined by laws, but prose wanders on a freer road. For the public road of prose admits carts and wagons at random; the narrow path of a poetic line does not want such gross things, but rather expressions of a slender form, lest it be tarnished by the bulk of an unwieldy word. The meter must come like a little lady of the house, hair bound, cheeks shining, body slender, form beautiful. No series can be of such sweetness to the ear as the delightful comeliness of meter. Prosaic verse is grosser; it loves all words indiscriminately... . Otherwise the plan does not vary: the art is ever the same, whether it be in verse bound by the laws of meter, or discourse free from those restrictions. However, what depends on the art is not always the same. In both prose and verse let the words be tamed. Let them not be dry, but let the sentence squeeze juice out of them. Let them be full of juice and blood, lest they seem puerile in any way.)

31 Both text and translation are from Ernest Gallo, *The Poetria Noga and its Sources in Early Rhetorical Doctrine* (Paris: Mouton, 1971), pp. 114-115.

6. Evrard l'Allemand (from *Laborintus,* early thirteenth century) [32]

Grammaticae famulans subit ingeniosa Poesia:
Officii confert ulterioris onus.
Explicat haec legem metri, quid pes docet, addens
Quid tempus, quot sint tempora cuique pedi,
Ex quot syllabicis constet pes partibus, et quae
Festinans, quae sit syllaba tarda docet.
Quis et quot pedibus constet lex quaeque metrorum
Et per quot genera sit variata docet.
Quod diversa metro non describuntur eodem.
Sed res quaeque suo sit proprieta docet.
Historias habet hexametrum, servitque querelae
Pentametrum, laudes cetera metra canunt.

(The serving of Grammar submits to ingenious Poesy; it joins the burden of the higher office. It explains the law of meter, what the foot teaches, giving the time, how many are the tempora to each foot, of how many syllabic parts the foot consists, and teaches which are the hurrying, and which the slow syllables; the law of which shows the kind and quantity constituting the feet, and through how many kinds of meters it is varied. Diverse kinds of poetry are not arranged in the same kind of meter, but the subject matter teaches what is appropriate. The hexameter holds for histories, the pentameter serves the complaint, the rest of the meters sing praises.)

7. From *Discantus positio vulgaris* (ca. 1230-1240) [33]

Aliquando vero tenor constat ex notis omnibus longis, sicut tenor motheti: *O Maria maris stella.* Et tunc semper nota longa cum brevi de motheto, uni tantum note longe de tenore correspondet, et e converso.

. . . . .

Aliquando vero disconvenit constans, scilicet ex omnibus longis, et tunc semper totum primo modo sit oppositum; in pausis tamen utrisque conveniunt.

32 Faral, *opere citato,* pp. 345-346.
33 Edmund de Coussemaker, *Scriptorum de Musica Medii Aevi* (Paris: A. Durand, 1864), I,96.

(Sometimes a tenor consists of all long notes, like the tenor of the motet *O Maria maris stella;* and then a long note always corresponds with a short one of the motetus, corresponds to one such long nate of the tenor, and the converse.

. . . . .

Sometimes the invariable is inconsistent, that is to say, consists of all longs and yet the whole of it is always put in first mode; in rests, however, both parts coincide.)

8. Pseudo-Aristotle or Lambert (from *Tractatus de Musica,* ca. 1240) [34]

> Primus modus dicitur, qui tantum componitur perfectis figuris, ut monstrat qui sequitur cantus qui colligitur ex perfectis puris:

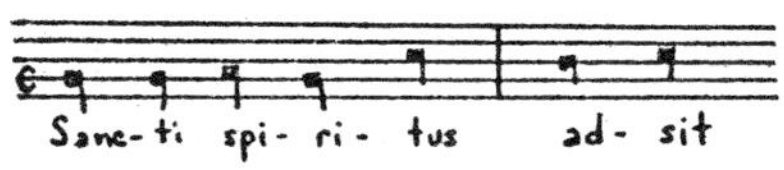

> Et hoc patet igitur quod nunquam comprimitur in ligaturis, sed liber excipitur, et solus non patitur unquam a pressuris; regit et non regitur, imperans non utitur aliorum curis:

> Iste primus dicitur et juste preponitur aliis venturis; nam ad hunc reducitur, et in hunc resolvitur quivis ex futuris.

(The first mode is said to be that which is composed of perfect figures, as demonstrates the following chant which is arranged from perfect pure notes:

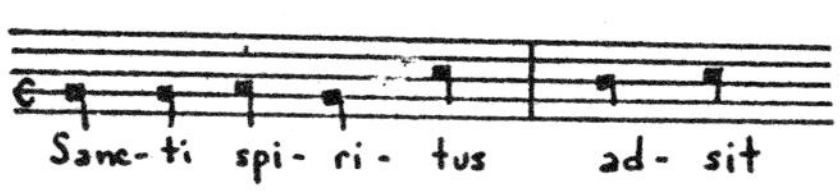

34 Edmund de Coussemaker, *Scriptorum de Musica Medii Aevi* (Paris: A. Durand, 1864), I,279.

And it is allowed, therefore, that it never be compressed in ligatures, rather, the text is taken up, and a single note is not ever allowed to escape from measuring; it governs but is not governed; commanding, it is not used with the care of others:

It is called the first mode and is rightly put before others that were to come; for anything that came later can be reduced to it and resolved in it.) [35]

9. Jerome of Moravia quoting Isidore of Seville (from the *Tractatus de Musica,* ca. 1250) [36]

> Rithmica est que requirit incurtionem verborum, utrum sonus bene aut male cohereat. Metrica est, que mensuram diversorum metrorum probabili ratione cognoscit, ut verbi gratia: heroicum, iambicum, elegiacum, etc.

(Rhythm is that which requires a beating of the words, [and determines] whether the sound adheres well or badly. Metrics is that which decides the probable measure of diverse meters; as for example, heroic, iambic, elegiac, etc.)

10. Anonymous IV (from *De Mensuris et Discantu,* ca. 1275) [37]

> Omnis simplex figura, prout se ostendit sub suo nomine, elongatur vel abbreviatur. Distractio est propter syllabas subpositas, quoniam supra quamlibet syllabam quandoque ponitur, una simplex sibi ipsi attribuitur. Et ratione diversitatis syllabarum, secundum aliquos, quilibet punctus absolutus dicitur, prout non reducitur ad figuram ligata.
>
> . . . . .

35 The illustration *Sancti spiritus adsit* is the beginning of a sequence by Notker Balbulus.

36 Coussemaker, *Scriptorum,* I, 7.

37 *Ibidem,* pp. 343-344.

... erant primo confuse quoad notitiam, sed per modum equivocationis accipiebantur, quod quidem modo non est, quoniam in antiquis libris habebant puncta equivoca nimis, quia simplicia materialia fuerunt equalia, sed solo intellectu operabantur dicendo: intelligo istam longam, intelligo illam brevem, et nimio tempore longo laborabant, antequam scirent bene aliquid quod nunc ex levi ab omnibus laborantibus circa talia percipitur mediantibus predictorum, ita quod quilibet plus proficeret in una hora quam in septem ante quoad longum ire.

Maxima pars cognitionis antiquorum fuit in predictis sine materiali significatione... .

(Every single note, according to how it shows itself under its name, is elongated or abbreviated. The fragmenting of ligatures is on account of the syllables placed underneath, since above whatever syllable it is placed, and whenever, a single note is attributed to it. And by the reckoning of the diversity of syllables, according to some, those which are called absolute notes accordingly are not reduced to ligatures.

. . . . .

[Ligatures with propriety and without perfection] were at first confused in conception, but through a manner of equivocation were accepted. In the ancient books, the notes were too equivocal, because the notation was not discrete; the old masters worked it out by intellect alone, saying: "I know that this is a long, and that a breve." Thus they worked a long time before they learned something which today anybody can easily learn by means of what has been said above. Thus today, more can be accomplished in an hour than in what formerly took seven. A great part of the cognition of the ancients was determined in prior discussion without the material significance of notation... . [He goes on to mention a time just before Perotin during which notation was reformed.]

11. Walter Odlngton (from *De Speculatione Musicae,* ca. 1300) [38]

Rhythmus non est certo fine moderatus; sed tamen rationabiliter ordinatis pedibus currit. Pedes sunt qui certis syllabarum temporibus insistunt. Et tempus quidem est mensura motus syllabe, ut cum solum pulsum habeat syllabe, ut cum solum pulsum habeat syllaba, dicatur longa et duorum temporum.

38 Coussemaker, *Scriptorum,* I, 211.

(Rhythm is not regulated by a fixed limit; but nevertheless it runs rationally according to the appointed feet. Feet are those things which are based upon the fixed times of syllables. And indeed, a tempus is the measure of movement of a syllable such that when a syllable holds a solitary pulse, it is long and of two tempora. [There follows a detailed description of poetic feet and their temporal measurement.])

12. Johannes de Grocheo (from *De Musica,* ca. 1300) [39]

> Et in alleluia additur cauda quaedam, sicut neupma in antiphonis. Et multoties loco caudae cantatur sequentia, puta cum missa celebratur cum maiori sollemnitate.
>
> Est autem sequentia cantus ex pluribus versiculis compositus, sicut *Laetabundus* vel *Benedicta es, caelorum.* Cantus autem iste per tonos regulatur sicut alii. Et duo versiculi sese sequentes in eadem concordantia ut plurimum decantantur.
>
> Iste autem tres cantus, puta responsorium, alleluia et sequentia, cantantur immediate post epistolam et ante evangelium in mysterio et reverentia trinitatis. Responsorium autem et alleluia decantantur ad modum stantipedes vel cantus coronati, ut devotionem et humilitatem in cordibus auditorum imponant. Sed sequentia cantatur ad modum ductiae, ut rectae recipiant verba novi testamenti, puta sacrum evangelium, quod statim postea decantatur.
>
> Et missa aliquoties est sine alleluia et sequentia, puta tempore luctus vel paenitentiae, et loco istorum cantatur tractus, qui est cantus ex versibus aggregatus. Cuiusmodi est *De profundis* vel *Sicut cervus.*
>
> . . . . .
>
> Ductia vero est cantilena levis et velox in ascensu et descensu, quae in choreis a iuvenibus et puellis decantatur, sicut gallice *A l'entrant d'amors* vel *Certes mie cuidoie.* Haec autem facit animos iuvenum et puellarum propter sui difficultatem circa hanc stare et eos a prava cogitatione devertit.
>
> . . . . .

39 Ernst Rohloff, *Die Quellenhandschriften zum Musiktraktat des Johannes de Grocheo* (Leipzig: VEB Deutscher Verlag für Musik, 1967), pp. 162, 132, and 134.

> Est autem ductia sonus illiteratus, cum decenti percussione mensuratus. Dico autem illiteratus, quia, licet in voce humana fieri possit et per figuras repraesentari, non tamen per litteras scribi potest, quia littera et dictamine caret. Sed cum recta percussione, eo quod ictus eam mensurant et motum facientis et excitant animum hominis ad ornate movendum secundum artem, quam ballare vocant, et eius motum mensurant in ductiis et choreis.

(And in the alleluia there is added a kind of cauda, much like the *neupma* in antiphons. Frequently, the sequence is sung in place of this cauda, that is, when Mass is celebrated with greater solemnity.

The sequence is a song composed of many versicles, just as *Laetabundus* or *Benedicta es celorum.* This song is ruled by the tones [modes], just like the others. And, as much as possible, two versicles following one another are sung in the same concordance [i. e., are musically identical].

These three songs, however, the responsory, alleluia, and sequence, are sung immediately after the epistle and before the evangel in mystery and reverence for the Trinity. The responsory and alleluia are sung after the fashion of the *stantipes* or *cantus coronatus,* in order that they might impose devotion and humility in the hearts of those listening. But the sequence is sung after the fashion of the ductia, so that it might lead and make joyful, so that the words of the New Testament, that is, the Holy Evangel, which is sung immediately afterwards, they might correctly receive.

And the Mass is sometimes without alleluia and sequence, as in the time of grief or penitence, and in its place is sung the tract, which is a song joined from verses. Of this type is the *De profundis* or *Sicut cervus.*

. . . . .

The ductia is a cantilena, light and swift in ascent and descent, which is sung in chorus by youths and girls, such as the French *A l'entrant d'amors* or *Certes mie ne cuidoie.* This influences the minds of young men and ladies and diverts them from improper thinking.

A ductia is also an untexted composition, measured with an appropriate drum beat. I say untexted because it is permissible to do it with the human voice and it is possible to write it in notation, nevertheless, it is impossible to describe it in words because it lacks vocabulary and method. But with a correct percussiveness, in that which measures it and the movements of the performers, it excites the spirit of men to moving ornately according to that art which they call dancing, and they measure its motion in ductias and choruses.)

At this point it would be tedious to paraphrase the above excerpts, since the translations already served that purpose, but the salient points must be extracted and threads followed through the labyrinth.

"No writer had a more persistent influence on the higher ranges of medieval thought," than Augustine. [40] The quotation from Augustine above—a small sampling of many such instances in his dialogues—proves conclusively that he conceived of poetic feet in terms of variable quantity rather than in accentual or equal rhythms. [41] It immediately casts doubt upon statements by philologists which imply that poetic meter (and by extension the musical meter of syllabically-set poetry) in the Middle Ages was purely accentual. [42] Similarly, the equalist interpretation of Gregorian chant rhythm maintained by Solesmes, although possibly of some merit in respect to music with prose texts or in neumatic or melismatic setting, would also appear to be inappropriate in application to sequences. The enormous number of quantified poetic meters and their mixture described by Augustine constitute a most appropriate foundation for the classical sequence, a syllabically based genre diversified in most of its elements. This diversity also extended to the mixing of metrical patterns. [43]

The quantitative meter described by Augustine and confirmed later by Isidore, although still mixed by Guido's time, must have been perpetuated through the twelfth century; but it became increasingly simplified and pervasively uniform. Matthieu de Vendôme, Geoffrey of Vinsauf, and Evrard l'Allemand, three rhetoricians who included poetry in their studies, confirm that poetic feet were still measured quantitatively in the twelfth century, but they also betray a disenchantment

40 C. M. Haskins, *The Renaissance of the Twelfth Century* (Cambridge, Mass.: Harvard University Press, 1927), p. 80.

41 Also see William Waite, *The Rhythm of Twelfth-Century Polyphony* (New Haven: Yale University Press, 1954), pp. 29-40.

42 For more on this, see Gillingham, *A History of the Polyphonic Sequence in the Middle Ages,* pp. 54-85.

43 *Ibidem.*

with the past. Matthieu, writing at about the same time that the music of the eleventh fascicle of W_1 was composed, explains the poetic feet of the "moderns" in terms of strict rules derived from the modus and tempus of syllables in poetry, and is supported by the other two. Evrard mentions the "hurrying" and "slow" syllables of poetry, and that the kind of meter to be chosen depends on the type and content of the poem. All sustain the view that poetry was unequally quantified according to rules which departed from the abuses of the "ancients"; these abuses may have included the mixing of poetic feet.

From these accounts, and the later more thorough ruminations of Walter Odington, it can be confidently maintained that poetic meter was conceived quantitatively, not equally or accentually. But did this quantification extend to the music (which was not metrically specific in its notation)? The author of *Discantus positio vulgaris* and Pseudo-Aristotle (Lambert) appear to answer yes to the question; the latter even employs a portion of a sequence notated in equal longs to illustrate his views—the implication being that it would have been unequally quantified in performance. Syllables underneath music can replace ligatures and provide mensuration, according to Anonymous IV, who also mentions a time before Perotin, probably in the third quarter of the twelfth century or before, when notation was not a significant indicator of rhythm; it is just about at that time when the sequences from W_1 were composed. In the last quotation above, Johannes de Grocheo informs us about the purpose, character, and manner of performance of the sequence. Too frivolous for performance in church during Lent, when it was replaced by the tract, it was like the secular ductia, presumably measured with a percussive dance-like beat. Furthermore, light and swift ascent and descent were frequent earmarks of thirteenth-century sequences, and of those in W_1.

The style of the sequences in W_1 is dualistic in that the tenors and upper parts differ in their musical relationship to the text. Only the tenors, set in square notation in predominantly syllabic style and consisting mostly *ex omnibus longis* (with occasional ligatures) like most monophonic sequences of the period, preserve an intimate relationship with the text, In fact, the tenor setting is so intimate that the second half of the text of each double versicle is written in the margin without notation. The upper parts, in contrast, though aligned in score with the tenors and not floridly melismatic as in Parisian organa, are in a neumatic or group style. Since the sequences are neither in the organal nor in the conductus style of Notre Dame, the transcriptional procedures established for the music of Leonin and Perotin cannot automatically be applied. [44]

44 That is, as in Waite, *opere citato;* and Anderson, "The Rhythm of *cum lit-*

For the benefit of the sceptics, it must be demonstrated first that the notation, in the words of Anonymous IV, is not "materially significant" as to rhythm. The most telling indicator of modal rhythm—regular grouping and patterning of ligatures—is almost completely lacking,[45] as the grouping of ligatures in the upper-parts changes with every syllable, except for an occasional transitory repetition, and the groups themselves range from one to six notes in the upper part for every note (or ligature) of the tenor. Below are a number of vertical combinations which recur from time to time in the W_1 sequences.

Example 1. Common verticalities in the W_1 sequences.

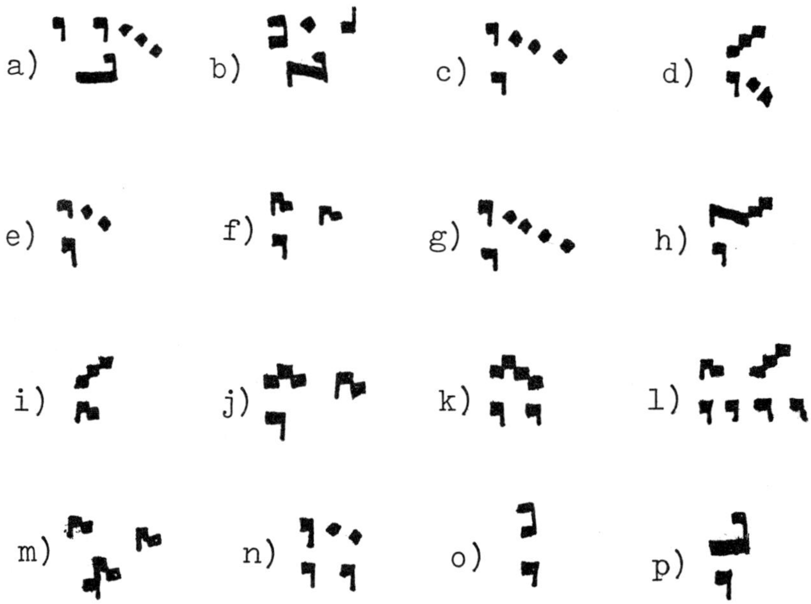

tera Sections of Polyphonic Conductus in Mensural Sources," *The Journal of the American Musicological Society,* XXVI (1973), 288-304.

45 Except for a few isolated spots in the final *Amens*.

In this notation, longs and plicas constitute the bulk of the notae simplices; breves and isolated semibreves occur less seldom (but both do appear),[46] the later being grouped most often in *currentes* or *conjuncturae* (see Frontispiece). The ligatures must be equivalent in meaning to the *currentes* since a ligature of two, three, or four notes in one voice often matches metrically a *currens* of the same number of notes in the other (see Example 1, d). The *conjuncturae* are favoured for descending motion whereas the ligatures are preferred for ascending or changing motion. In additon to the above, curious relationships between single notes of the tenor and other combinations in the upper part are not uncommon: 

In other words, a long, breve, or semibreve in one voice can equal a wide variety of notes, ligatures, or currentes in the other:

If it is assumed that the longae, even just those in the tenor, have a fixed value, then contradictions such as this arise:

Consequently, any note or group of notes can be made equal to any other note or ligature, therefore none of the note shapes has a fixed value. The notation on its own, although very accurate and careful in pitch, is ambiguous, variable, inconsistent, and even careless in its reflection of the rhythm, and it is the added part above the tenor that reveals this, for such rhythmic ambiguity is neither implicit nor explicit in the notation of contemporary monophonic counterparts.

Since the notation is inadequate in its provision for rhythm, guidance must be sought elsewhere. The investigation can be broken down into two parts: 1) the rhythm of the tenor, and 2) the rhythm of the upper parts. The tenor (as in monophonic sequences of the period) follows the syllabification of the text intimately, with only occasional ligatures, most of which are *binariae* or *ternariae.* Since, as stated

46 The later terminology is used only for convenience of reference to the note shapes, not in the mensural sense that a *brevis* is short and a *longa,* long in duration. Two other sporadic features of the notation are the archaic quilisma () and the binaria with exaggerated prolongation of the first note (). The former would seem to be ornamental in significance, while the latter probably indicates an extension of the expected duration.

earlier, there is good reason to believe that sequence texts and music had always been quantitatively realized according to poetic feet, it also makes sense to adapt the W_1 tenors to textual quantification. The majority of the sequences in W_1 are of the regular type in the standard trochaic metrical patterns (8/7, 8/8/7, and 8/8/8/7). Their tenors, therefore would best be transcribed in proto-first-mode, either in $^{6}/_{4}$ ) or $^{6}/_{8}$ (), but the former is preferable owing to the frequency of currentes in the upper voices and their resultant small note values. First mode rhythm works perfectly for the regular sequences, but not always for the other sequence types; however, the same principles can be applied if the correct poetic meter can be discovered (which it can), and this system for resolving the rhythm of the tenors, both in polyphony and monophonic guise, would seem to be not only the most rational and sensible, but also the most justified, considering the evidence quoted earlier from contemporary or nearly-contemporary sources. The system also explains why tenors (always the most conservative voice) in thirteenth-century clausulae and motets could be written in equal notes () which had various rhythmic meanings ( etc.).

The guiding principle in transcribing the upper voices, which are more flexible and ambiguous owing to the greater number of neumatic groups or melismas, is to adjust them to the tenors. When a note in the tenor is long (the longae in this music are generally two beats (), but are occasionally three (), a ligature above it must be spread out to take up the full two (or three) beats; when it is short (i. e., ), the upper melisma must cover one beat. This means that identical ligatures or *currentes* in the upper part can have different meanings according to their position over long or short notes in the tenor. The high proportion of binary-grouped ligatures and *currentes* (mainly in two's and four's), the equivalence of some ligatures (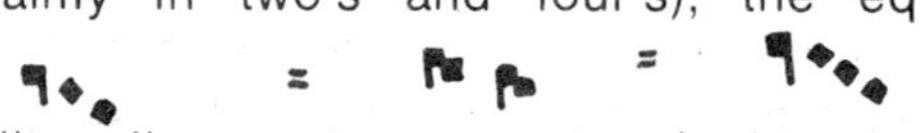), and the necessity for flexibility, all seem to suggest a duple subdivision of the prevailing triple meter. When inequality must result, as in some ternariae and quinariae, the largest note values should be reserved for the ends of groups (e. g.,

)

(in accordance with the theorists).[47]

47 For more on this, see Willi Apel, *The Notation of Polyphonic Music* (Cam-

One thorny problem remains before the present system of transcription may be considered complete, and that is the matter of determining the underlying poetic meter of a given sequence. As subsequent analysis will show, the four main types of sequences—classical, transitional, regular, and mature—are represented in the group of sequences from W_1. It is probably no coincidence that the most difficult to transcribe are the classical and transitional ones, since they manifest all the irregularities in phrasing, sectional length, and rhythmic patterning which have already been discussed, albeit with some modification or "regularization". That it is not possible to realize them with the same degree of certainty as the regular sequences tends to support the view that rhythm progressed from irregular quantification to regular. It should be born in mind that because the meters are difficult to retrieve now could also mean that they were then, for the compilers may also have had some difficulties in reviving the rhythms of the older sequences, since in some cases they were exploiting tenors up to three centuries old. Thus they may have used them quite cognizant of the original rhythms, which they tried to reproduce faithfully, or they may have attempted to simplify them to some kind of iambo-trochaic mix (the excesses of the "ancients" were not allowed by the "moderns"), [48] forcing them onto the Procrustean bed of current fashion. There is one guide in the notation, fortunately, which provides a solution.

The notation is similar throughout all fourteen pieces and gives little indication as to note values, except for one important aid, the *Silbenstrich (divisio modi),* which is particularly helpful in transcribing them all. The vertical slashes which pepper the manuscript recur predictably after groups of four and eight syllables in the acatalectic lines of the regular sequences, and after seven in the catalectic lines. In the irregular sequences their appearance is frequent but less consistent. In both types they usually occur at the beginning or end of a word and/or a group of words. The *Silbenstriche* do not indicate rests. This is evident, not only from concordant versions of pieces such as *Verbum bonum et suave* and *Virgini Mariae,* which have no (or far fewer) vertical slashes in other manuscripts, but also from internal evidence in the W_1 manuscript. If they are interpreted as rests they shred the music into incoherent and incomplete phrases. Then again, they sometimes encompass several short words on the first time through a double ver-

bridge, Mass.: The Mediaeval Academy of America, 1953), p., 241; and Waite, *opere citato,* pp. 86-88.

48 See the remarks of Matthieu de Vendôme on pp. 9-10.

sicle, but corresponding words for the second time, written in the margin, are longer and fewer in number (e. g., two groups of four syllables can become one group of eight in the repeat); rests would therefore break up the words in the repeat. Finally, the upper or lower voice sometimes exhibits a slash while the other does not, in places where coincidence of the parts is essential.

In this kind of music, where the notes of the tenor are so closely bound to the text, rests would not be necessary since catalexis in the poetry provides them, and hence, at this stage, the *Silbenstriche* are better viewed not as implying rests, but as guides clarifying the alignment of the voices, word-markers, and most important, syllable-counters. There is a direct relationship between the syllabic structure and the type of meter employed in other mensurally-notated sequences of the thirteenth century. [49] When odd- and even-numbered syllable groups are combined (e. g., 8/8/7 or 7/7/6) or odd-numbered groups repeated (e. g., 7/7/7/7) in these later sequences, the rhythm is trochaic or first mode; when the groupings are even (e. g., 6/6/6 or 8/8/8/8/8) the meter is invariably iambic or second mode. It is the opinion of the present writer that these relationships can safely be extrapolated back to the W_1 sequences and others like them which are indiscretely notated, or in other words, that the syllable grouping can be relied upon to furnish the correct poetic and musical meter. The practical results of the application of this theory may be evaluated in the transcriptions at the end of this study. [50]

An outstanding feature of the fourteen W_1 sequences—one reminiscent of the monophonic sequences of Nicolaus of Clairvaux[51]—is the inclusion of ten final melismatic Amens, all of which are for two voices (it is not clear whether or not their tenors were pre-existent but the latter seems most likely). There are three distinct types; in the first, the word Amen is placed under all or part of the final versicle, or written in the margin with no notation above, with the implication that the music of the final versicle be used; the second, which is notated in full, con-

49 For a more detailed discussion of mensurally notated sequences of the thirteenth century, see Gillingham, *opere citato,* pp. 180-237; and idem, "Modal Rhythm and the Medieval Sequence," *Studies in Music at the University of Western Ontario,* I (1976), 105-123.

50 The association of *Silbenstriche* with catalectic feet may well have led to their later function as rests; in any case, their usage results in the division of modal rhythmic patterns into ordines, a practice which was to become more explicit. Further metrical refinements are discussed in the Editorial Note below.

51 For more on this, see John Benton, "Nicolaus of Clairvaux and the Twelfth-Century Sequence," *Traditio,* XVIII (1962), 149-179.

sists of a very brief roulade after the sequence proper; and the third type, independently notated and grouped by *Silbenstriche*, is more extended. Three of the five irregular sequences (classical and transitional) have no Amen, one has a brief roulade *(Ave Maria gratia plena*, f. 185-185_v), [52] and one *(Reginarum dominam*, ff. 189_v-190) bears the sign "ꝑ" in the last versicle, indicating that the unnotated Amen in the margin should be sung to the concluding part of the versicle. None of the five has extended independent Amens divided by slashes, and hence one is led to the conclusion that the classical and transitional sequences were not suitable for extended *Amens*. The reason might well have been that the inconsistent rhythmic patterning in the sequence proper did not lend itself to extension.

The procedure differs in the case of the regular and mature sequences; seven out of the nine finish with more extended, independently notated *Amen*s, most of which are divided by *Silbenstriche*. Of the two without *Amens*, one *(Ave mundi spes Maria*, f. 186-186_v) concludes with the phrase *Amen dicat omnis homo* and thus to follow it with another *Amen* would have been redundant; in the other *(Ave caeli imperatrix*, f. 190) the *Amen* is unnotated in the margin and perhaps would have been sung to the music of the final versicle. Since so many end with them, we must conclude, therefore, that the regular and mature sequences were suited for extended, independent *Amens*. The probable reason is that their meter was consistent enough to be extended automatically without text, whereas the same cannot be said of the irregular sequences.

Verbum bonum et suave concludes with one of the more extended *Amens* in the W_1 sequence group.

Example 2. A reproduction of the final *Amen* in *Verbum bonum et suave*. (W_1, f. 192.)

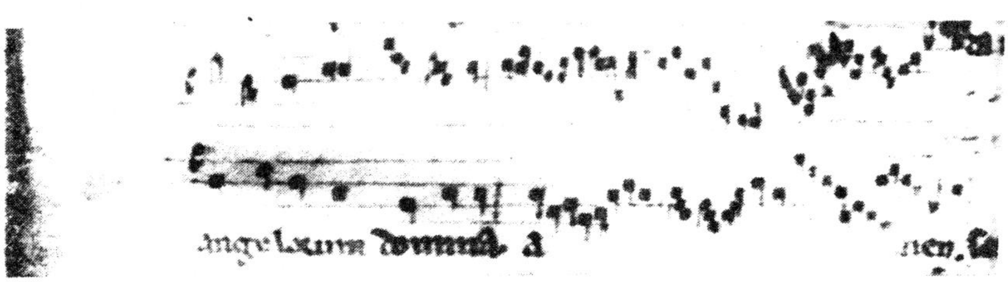

52 The last versicle is trochaic, however, and it is possible that its "regularity" should be extended to the *Amen* (i. e., that the first mode rhythm should be continued).

Musically the tenor duplicates the full final versicle of the sequence proper (see transcription No. 14) except that in the second phrase, three melodic skips of a third are filled in with passing notes (e. g.,  becomes  If texted, each of the three ligatures in question would have to account for two syllables, and thus would have to be broken; but since there was no reason to restrict ligation to a part of a foot, in other words, to match one syllable to one note or ligature, in melismatic setting, the ligatures have been extended to cover the whole poetic foot (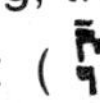). Eight longae comprise the first and third phrase of the Amen tenor; both phrases are equivalent to eight syllables. The second phrase, consisting of three *ternariae* (each the equivalent of two syllables) and two *longae,* is also eight syllables in length. The final phrase (with a plica counting as two syllables) is seven syllables long. The melismatic *Amen* thus replicates exactly the syllabic structure of all the other versicles in the sequence (it e., 8/8/8/7), and hence we may conclude, firstly, that a ligature in a melismatic passage could incorporate a whole poetic foot, and secondly, that the prevailing trochaic sequence meter was extended into the *Amen.*

A similar instance occurs in *Laudes Christo decantemus,* whose *Amen* contains the most extended passage of ligature repetition in the whole collection:

Example 3. The final *Amen* of *Laudes Christo decantemus.* (W_1, f. 188.)

Here, as in most of the other independent *Amens,* there is no pitch concordance between the Amen tenor and the preceding sequence proper. For the first three ordines the tenor progresses in equal groups of four notes each, with a ternaria or quaternaria in the upper voice for every two longae of the tenor. This much can be assumed to be an extension of the preceding regular meter, with the *ternariae* and *quaternaria* filling up the whole foot above the unequally divided foot of the tenor (i. e., 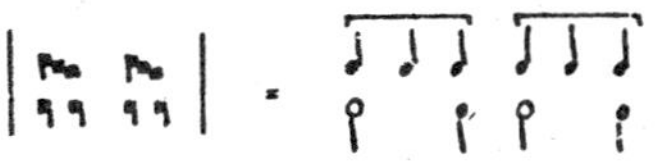). Then follow two ordines seemingly in the ligature arrangement of the first mode (3, 2, 2, . . .), that is, with the more florid ligatures of the upper part now extended to the tenor. But the notation is deceptive. The syllabic arrangement of the single versicles of poetry before the Amen is 8/8/7 which has been subdivided by *Silbenstriche* into 4/4/4/4/7 throughout most of the sequence. The tenor of the Amen begins with three ordines of four longs each (videlicet, 4/4/4—); the fifth ordo is made up of seven longs; if the fourth ordo is adapted to the equivalent of four syllables (which it easily can be), the implicit syllabification is again 4/4/4/4/7, but followed by a concluding roulade over a prolonged note in the tenor.[53] The ligature patterning in the fourth and fifth ordines, which is not identical, would therefore not appear to indicate notated first mode, but is an adaptation to the already established regular rhythm. If interpreted "as notated" in the first mode these ordines would constitute an anomalous departure from the rest of the piece that would spoil the greater symmetry. The extension of the internal rhythm of the texted sequence to these concluding melismata represents a crucial step on the road to notated modal rhythm and to florid mensural music. All that remained was to invest the notation itself with more specific meaning.

Of the fourteen W_1 sequences, two are "classical," three are transitional, two are mature, and the remaining seven are regular; in other words, roughly fourteen percent are classical, twenty-one percent transitional, fourteen percent mature, and fifty percent regular.[54] It should be emphasized that the classical, transitional, and mature sequences reveal clear signs of being modified or "regularized;" there has been a demonstrable attempt to adapt them to the symmetry and trochaic meter of the regular sequence. Nevertheless, the varied contents highlight the risks involved in attempting to date and establish provenance of sequences according to their poetic or musical style. No single region of Europe can be pinpointed as the home of the sequence texts, but the Victor, and others to specific localities such as St. Martial, would seem to indicate French origins; but this does not mean that they were not ex-

53 See transcription No. 7.

54 For a more detailed analysis, see Commentary.

ported abroad. Three of the sequences (Nos. 6, 7, and 10) for certain are textual parodies with tenors borrowed from their models, one was later parodied (No. 4), and the popular *Verbum bonum* (No. 14) may have been modelled or copied with a few alterations. The texts of the other sequences often contain minor departures (such as substitute words, rearrangement of the order of words and/or verses, etc.) from their textual concordances. There are disparities amongst the W_1 versions and those by Kehrein, and those in *Analecta Hymnica.* [55] Hence, it appears that most of the texts in the group were either modified on a large scale to suit the purpose of venerating the Virgin, or revised on a small scale for other reasons. They illustrate Matthieu de Vendôme's comment (pp. 9-10) that poetry could either be "modelled" or "freely-created." Originality evidently was not considered a prime virtue for sequentors.

Most of the sequences begin and end (i. e., before the added Amens) with double rather than single versicles, but three have single versicles at the beginning (Nos. 2, 7, and 10), and two at the end (Nos. 2 and 12). As might be expected, three out of five of these single versicles occur in classical sequence types. The texts (either modelled, newly created, or borrowed) and tenors (at least eleven of the fourteen seem to have pre-existent, and the other three—Nos. 9, 11, and 13—may also have been) largely determine the overall forms of the polyphonic elaborations, as well as some of the inner details such as cadences. Eight of the works are in Mixolydian mode, four in Dorian, and two in mixed modality. The monophonic preference for Mixolydian and Dorian is preserved in the polyphonic settings, but no one mode is peculiar to the classical, transitional, regular, or mature types in W_1. The prime consonances on strong beats are the octave, fifth, and unison, all of which are periodically intensified by a sprinkling of upward and downward resolving appoggiaturas (frequently sevenths). Thirds on strong beats, which might be expected if the pieces were English, seldom occur. Contrary motion prevails in the voice-leading, with frequent interspersions of parallel and oblique motion.

55 The texts in the transcriptions have been presented as they appear in W_1 unless otherwise indicated in the Editorial Note.

Cadences can be discussed from the standpoint of the tenor alone or from that of the two voices together. In the former, the two most common patterns are the sequence cadence and the descending scale passage. Thus, not counting abridged or modified sequence cadences of which there are many, every piece except *Virgo mitis verae vitis* (No. 9) has at least one full sequence cadence, and *Laudes Christo decantemus* (No. 7) includes nine of them; in fact, there are thirty-two altogether within the fourteen examples—many of them decorated with a plica on the antepenultimate note. Descending scalar cadences of three notes or more occur with less frequency, as they appear in only eight of the fourteen sequences, and total seventeen in all. The most common resolution for the upper parts in cadences is an approach by contrary motion, concluding with a single note consonant with the final note of the tenor. However, the upper voice often decorates the last tenor note with assorted roulades or ornaments. In performance, these would undoubtedly require retardation and/or fermatas.

Example 4.
Various decorated cadences in the W_1 sequence group.

A few remarks, in conclusion, must be made about the wider ramifications of the theories and observations developed above. The addition, in the texted part of the sequences, of a melodically independent and more florid voice, compared to the tenor, and, in the Amens, the use of a florid melismatic style in both voices must have spurred composers to devise a less equivocal system of notation, namely, notated modal rhythm. Leonin only used one mode in his organum, the first, or "metrical trochee"; he would hardly have needed to turn back to Augustine for his inspiration as Waite suggests, for the metrical system inherent in the sequence (monophonic and polyphonic) of the mid-twelfth century, with its modal poetically-based trochaic structure, provided ample precedent. Like so many "innovations" in music, those of Leonin must have developed from practical forerunners, and all that remained for him to do was to re-apply pre-existent principles, and to refine and reduce rhythms from indiscrete *longae* given discrete meaning by a text, to discrete ligatures which could function without text. Although the accomplishment of Leonin cannot be denigrated, Waite's assessment of it as "revolutionary" must be discounted.[56]

If the rhythmic system described above is correct, even if in the twelfth century it was more flexible than the transcriptions might imply, then it has wide import for monophonic and polyphonic sequence-related genres such as the lai, estampie, and ductia, not to mention the conductus. Perhaps the principles could also be extended to some other kinds of chant, although such an extravagant claim is not fully justified without a thorough genre study of the different kinds of chant. In the twelfth-century sequence, not only the foundations for modal rhythm and later indiscretely notated tenors may be observed, but also the prototype for repeated tenors in clausula and motet. The small collection of sequences in W_1, neglected in past years, thus opens up possibilities of the utmost importance to the correct realization of an immense quantity of music.

56 For a discussion of Leonin's achievement, see Waite, *opere citato,* pp. 8-9.

COMMENTARY

An important first step in understanding the W_1 sequences is to assess the provenance, style, and meaning of their texts. Accordingly, they are numbered below (with foliation given), classified as to type, a stanza or two of each is scanned poetically, authors are cited when known, references to textual editions are provided (the only edition of the texts which is based exclusively on W_1 is the Milchsack edition), the texts are translated in a free prose style (it is virtually impossible to replicate the poetic structure of the originals in English), and additional comments offered when deemed necessary.

1. *Mittet ad virginem* (attributed to Peter Abelard), ff. 183_v-184.

Text: Analecta Hymnica, LIV, No. 191; Kehrein, No. 199; Milchsack, No. 231.

Scansion:

```
- v -  v -v- |
Mittit ad virginem
-    v  - v -v- |
Non quemvis angelum
-  v -v-v- |
Sed fortitudinem
-v   -  v  -v- |
Suam, archangelum
- v -  v -v- |
Amator hominis
```

Type: mature.

Translation: The lover of mankind sends to the Virgin, not just any angel, but his strong archangel. He would set free the strong messenger for us, so that he might make of creation a precedent for the childbirth of the Virgin.

[He did this so that] the King born of glory might surpass nature, that He might rule and command, and lift up the seeds of sin from our midst; that he might wear down the gable-ends of pride, trampling by force the near high hill, powerful in battle.

Go forth, you who are sent to announce these gifts. Unveil the covering of the old text by virtue of the messenger, so that he might cast out the worldly leader and make the mother, with him, sharer of the Father's command.

Approach, messenger. Face to face, say "Hail, thou art full of grace, the Lord be with thee, fear not. Virgin, submit to the deposition of God, for which you must hold to your purpose in chastity and keep your vow."

The maiden hears and accepts the message; she believes, conceives, and bears a son—a wonderful counsellor of human kind, a mighty God, peace in the future, firm in peace. He who allots to us pardon for sin, He who consciously washes it away, and sacrifices to the Father in the arch of the stars, imparting compassion to the accused and admitting servants, by the grace of the mother, admits consorts above. Amen.

Comment: On first glance it would appear that the meter should be either dactylic dimeter or iambic tetrameter, but the musical setting has clearly been modified to trochaic tetrameter catalectic (7/7/7/7/7) with an extra note being added over the penultimate syllable of each line. It is an unusual sequence not only because of its meter, but also because of its stanzaic structure and rhyme.[57]

2. Paranymphus salutat virginum, ff. 184-184$_{v}$.

Text: Analecta Hymnica, X, No. 88; Milchsack, No. 232.

- v-v | - v - v
Scansion: III, a O Maria, ne formides
- v - v | -v - v
Praebe fidem, quia fides
-v - v -v-
Potens in hoc opere.
v -v -v- |
V, a O puer sapiens
v - v -v- |
O verbum vagiens
- v - v -v-
O majestas humilis.

Type: late transitional (or early regular).

Translation: The bridesman greets the Virgin, sealing the arrangement of the new birth. "Behold," he says, "you shall conceive and bring forth a child, and you will not experience the damage of inchastity."

Now, anticipated grace, but also ignorant doubt, seeks an explanation of the matter.

Oh, Mary, lest you be frightened, show faith, because faith is powerful [in times] of trouble. Oh, Mary, be thou tranquil in assenting to the birth of God without the league of man!

The word is joined to flesh in the womb of the Virgin and birth does not remove one from the other. Oh, fortunate novelty! Oh, remarkable worthiness that the Deity lies in a narrow stall! Oh, wise boy! Oh, crying word! Oh, majestic humility! Help us, rule us, protect us by the word, in flesh similar to ours!

Oh, Mary, the mother of God, in thee breathes out hope of the thing; thou, after God, are the assurance of our faith.

57 See Gillingham, *A History of the Polyphonic Sequence,* p. 71 for more on this.

Jesus, holy! Jesus, strong! Jesus, leader of our resurrection! Make us to be of thy kind in glory! Hail, grace of the mother! Amen.

Comment: The appearance of this sequence in W_1 must be one of the earliest on record, since *Analecta Hymnica* dates it as thirteenth- or fourteenth-century. The irregularity in syllabification from stanza to stanza (a transitional characteristic) linked with the more forward-looking double rhyming (which is extensive) would seem to place the sequence on the borderline between transitional and regular (i. e., a compositional date of ca. 1100). The sequence appears later in the Worcester Fragments. [58]

3. *Ave Maria gratia plena,* ff. 185-185$_v$.

Text: Analecta Hymnica, LIV, No. 216; Kehrein, No. 264; Milchsack, No. 233.

v - v -v -v- v - ı
Scansion: Ave Maria gratia plena
v - v - v - v - v -
Dominus tecum virgo serena.

Type: transitional.

Translation: Hail, Mary, full of grace, the Lord be with thee, virgin bright; blessed art thou amongst women and blessed is the fruit of thy womb, from which thou hast brought forth peace to men and glory to the angels, thou who hast granted by grace that we might be thy coheirs.

By this "ave," however, so sweet to the world, you have created, contrary to the laws of the flesh, an offspring, new alone, under a newly-created star. You have functioned as the temple of the small and great, of the lion and the lamb, of Christ the saviour, but you are an untouched virgin. You, queen of flower and dew, of bread and herd, queen of virgins, rose without thorn, you have been made a mother. You are the city of royal justice, the mother of sorrows, shaping anew the Godly love of grace from the lake of mire and misery.

Therefore, may the star of the sea, the storehouse of God's word and dawn of the sun, the door of paradise through which light comes forth, both free us from sins and establish us forever in the kingdom of brilliancy, in which light shines on the earnest. Amen.

Comment: At one time the opening stanza may have been done in adonic verse (— v v — v | — v v — v), but in this version it appears to be iambic with succeeding stanzas adopting still other meters. [59] On f. 185, on the system immediately above the bottom one, there is an early example of the use of the "g" clef, the only such instance in the collection.

58 Luther Dittmer, *The Worcester Fragments* (Rome: The American Institute of Musicology, 1957), No. 106.

59 Karl Bartsch, *Die lateinischen Sequenzen des Mittelalters* (Hildesheim: Georg Olms, 1968), p. 195.

4. *Hodierne lux diei,* ff. 185_v-186.

Text: Analecta Hymnica, LIV, No. 219; Kehrein, Nos. 202 and 498; Milchsack, No. 234.

- v- v - v-v ı
Scansion: Hodiernae lux diei
- v - v -v -v ı
Celebris in viri Dei
- v- v -v-
Agitur memoria;

Type: regular (8/8/7).

Translation: The honoured light of this day is passed in memory of the mother of God; on this day let us ever sing the praises and laudations of the Virgin Mary.

Each man to each entreat and implore her at the appointed hour for her protection! Sing! Play! in the full flight of string, voice, in word and in prayer:hail [Mary] full of grace. Hail, mistress of the heavens, [you who are] unacquainted with the couch of a man, parent without equal; daughter fruitful without a man, in a wonderous way, you have created a creator! You are a flowering garden by the south wind fanned, a closed door after and before, a path untrod by a man, soil flowering with the dew of heaven, the outspread fleece of Gideon, the rain of deity.

Hail, splendor of the firmament. You gleeming illuminator of foggy minds from above. Calm the sea, star of the sea, lest tempest and the ready storm roll over us. Amen.

Comment: In a later St. Gall source, a few words have been changed *(Antoni, Paduana* substituted for *omni hora* and *cordis ora* respectively, and a few other alterations) and the sequence used as a tribute to St. Anthony of Padua (1195-1231). According to Analecta Hymnica, LIV, xiv, the W_1 version of the text already existed in the eleventh century. It must therefore be assumed that the St. Anthony version was a parody, not the reverse.

5. *Ave mundi spes Maria,* ff. 186-186_v.

Text: Analecta Hymnica, LIV, No. 217; Kehrein, No., 289; Milchsack, No. 235.

- v - v - v -v ı
Scansion: Ave mundi spes Maria
- v -v -v -v ı
Ave mitis ave pia
- v - v - v-
Ave plena gratia;

Type: regular (8/8/7).

Translation: Hail, Mary, hope of the world; hail gentle, hail holy, hail Mary full of grace! Hail, unique Virgin! Hail, worthy star of the sea, filling the world with glory! Hail, beautiful rose! Hail, rod of Jesse, whose fruit looses the bonds of our grief.

Hail, you whose flesh issued a son in opposition to the covenant of death! Hail, you, without resemblance, who long ago restored joy to the wretched world! Hail, lamp of virgins through which heavenly light shone on those who clung to darkness! I hail you from whom the King of heavens was ordained to be born and on whose milk He was to feed!

Hail, gem of the heavenly windows!

Hail, sacristy of the Holy Spirit!

Oh, how laudable and how wonderful is this virginity, in which fruitfulness, brought about by the Hoty Spirit, shone.

Oh, how worthy, how serene, how benign, how pleasant are you from whom Christ was born; by whom slavery is ended, the gate of heaven opened, and liberty returned.

Oh, lily of chastity, entreat your Son, who is the salvation of the humble, that he not, in wretched judgment, cast us down in punishment for our sins; but, by your holy prayer, cleansing us from the mire of sin, settle us in the home of light! May every man say, "Amen."

Comment: Versicles II and IX drop the second line of text.

6. *Virgini Mariae laudes* (attributed to Adam of St. Victor), f. 187.

Text: Analecta Hymnica, LIV, No. 18; Kehrein, No. 234; Milchsack, No. 236. - v- v-v - v|- v - v - v-

Scansion: Virgini Mariae laudes intonent Christiani

Type: transitional.

Translation: Let Christians intone praises to the Virgin Mary. Eve Broght misery, but Mary contributed to the birth of Him who delivers sinners. Law and virtue were united in a wonderful way:the son of Mary reigns as God.

Tell us, Mary, virgin merciful and holy—"the angel, a witness, was sent to me from heaven"—when you were the shaper of God's birth, how was a mother made? "My hope was born of me, but unbelieving Judea [still] waits." Gabriel alone is more to be believed than the false crowd of Judeans.

We know that Christ truly came forth from Mary; thou born a king, pity us.

Comment: The meter is somewhat irregular, but much of it seems to have been "regularized" into trochaic. The piece is a parody of Wipo's transitional sequence, *Victimae paschali,* and thus adapts to the musical and textual irregularities of that work.

60 Supplied from *Analecta Hymnica,* VII, No. 101.

7. *Laudes Christo decantemus,* ff. 187-188.
Text: Analecta Hymnica, XXXIV, No. 143; Milchsack, Nos. 237-239

- v -v | - v -v |
Scansion: II, a Dulce melos pulset caelos
- v - v - v - v |
Nam benignam dulci digna
- v - v - v -
Credimus melodia;

Type: regular (8/8/7).

Translation: Let us sing praises to Christ, He who, in the special glory of His mother, we delight in. May sweet melody strike the heavens, for we believe that worthy melody is agreeable to the friendly. Life conforms to the voice in order that Mary, in memory, may be celebrated.

Let those, who rejoice in themselves to be given the gifts of life by her, praise the mother of the Saviour. Oh what a faithful and distinguished mother [she is], a virgin dear to God, filled with the sacred deity.

May each and every one say: "Hail, salvation of all people, virgin and mother." To the unspotted lamb, under the covering of flesh, she gave draughts of milk.

She is the ladder of sinners by which Christ, the King of heaven, descended to the world below; she through whose singular figure the secret gifts of the saving dew are given. She always makes her victors more steadfast, she heals the sick and feeble, and represses demons; she gives liberty to captives, contributes a freshness to life and dignity to the aged, and rescues everyone.

Virgin, special watchword, true salvation of the world, hail! Amongst the signs there is no such leaf, flower, [or] seed. Christian medicine, save the healthy, heal the sick!

Because human power is weak unless it be in your name, help us, holy Jesus, as we are taking up the praises of your mother, and transport the servants of your mother, after this life, to the palace of God the Father. In order that they will have the strength to serve your mother, prepare them not to feel bitterness. But when judgment day comes, confer and bestow on us eternal joy. Amen.

Comment: This sequence is a parody of *Laudes crucis attollamus* ascribed to Adam of St. Victor (see *Analecta Hymnica*, LIV, No. 120 and Misset-Aubry, No. XVIII). The purpose of the model was to venerate the cross; in this version, which includes substantial quotations from the model, the text has been revised to suit the prevailing Marian emphasis. The Milchsack version of the text is incorrect; he has split the sequence into three separate sequences (Nos. 237-239), and in the process, divorced parallel double versicles. For the sake of clarity, we will continue to use the Milchsack numbering.

8. *Missus Gabriel de caelis,* ff. 188_v-189.

Text: Analecta Hymnica, LIV, No., 192; Kehrein, No. 200; Milchsack, No. 240.

- v - v- v - v I
Scansion: Missus Gabriel de caelis
- v -v - v -v I
Verbi baiulus fidelis
- v - v - v - v I
Sacris disseret loquelis
- v- v - v -
Cum beata virgine;

Type: regular (8/8/8/7).

Translation: Sent from heaven, Gabriel, the faithful porter of the word, examines sacred words with the blessed Virgin. The good sweet word stretches out into the bedroom and from Eva forms an Ave by inverting the name of Eva; consequently, the bargain bound, the word is made flesh but the maidenhead is ever intact.

The birth knows no equal; a man does not deflower her, nor does the Son twist or labour when it is born. You have heard about the sign of newness; it is enough only to believe it; it is not for your faculties to loose the bootlace. The great and remarkable sign is in the bush and the fire; nor does anyone worthy approach supplied with shoes.

A dry rod without dew, in a new rite, a new manner, bore fruit with a flower, and thus the Virgin gave birth. Blessed is such fruit, fruit of joy, not of mourning; Adam would not have been seduced if he had tasted of this.

Our Jesus, good Jesus, holy burden of the holy mother, He whose throne is in heaven was born in a stable. He who was thus born for us destroys our misgivings, because our dwelling here is frought with peril. Amen.

Comment: None.

9. *Virgo mitis verae vitis,* f. 189.

Text: Milchsack, No. 241.

- v - v I - v - v I
Scansion: Virgo mitis verae vitis
- v - v - v-
Radix mater Maria.

Type: regular (8/7).

Translation: Virgin mild, root of the true vine, mother Mary, into whom came the King, He who alleviated the evil uncertainties of the world! The voice of the faithful Gabriel instructs her in that arrangement:the immeasurable King is made measurable through thee, virgin mother.

Oh maiden, shrine of God, temple of the Holy Spirit, by whom the world was made pleasant and restored to newness! In this open sea, virgin mother, free us from evil as we applaud and sing to thee above the stars. Amen.

Comment: This is the shortest sequence in the W_1 group and appears to have been unique to W_1.

10. *Reginarum dominam,* ff. 189_v-190.

Text: Analecta Hymnica, LIV, No. 23; Milchsack, No. 242.

Scansion:

- v - v - v - |
Reginarum dominam
- v - v - v - |
Laudemus gloriosam
v - v - v |
Quam matrem Dei
- v - v - v -
Nisu omnes adorant.

Type: classical.

Translation: Let us praise the glorious mistress of queens, that mother of the just God whom all adore.

Thousands rejoice in the boundless grace and wonder at the power; for she deserved to conceive a God who would come to save all nations. Divinity was disposed on Mary so that she could take on the figure of a servant: the King of kings, the God and creator of everything, the man who was made by Mary.

She enlightens the world, adorns heaven. Rising out of Jacob, the glittering star of the sea, the extremely powerful Virgin, crushes under foot the savage Leviathan serpent.

At the birth, the Magi bring gifts to Mary, at the same time, gold, frankincense, and myrrh; and they predict a little God, a mortal King, with their gold, frankincense, and myrrh.

Protect those who are praising thee, Virgin, from their enemies, and lead them to the heavenly kingdom. And let them offer prayers to thy family, Mary, in order to avoid the evil of the enemy. Amen.

Comment: This is a parody of the classical sequence *Epiphaniam Domino* (Analecta Hymnica, LIII, No. 28), and as such is highly irregular in meter.

11. *Ave, caeli imperatrix,* f. 190.

Text: Milchsack, No. 243.

Scansion:

- v - v - v - v |
Ave caeli imperatrix
- v - v - v - v |
Apud Deum mediatrix
- v - v - v -
Et adiutrix legium;

Type: regular (8/8/7).

Translation: Hail. governess of heaven, mediator in the presence of God, and helper of the nations; prepare, strengthen, and spread out your task, and, clement [Virgin], defend this colleagueship.

We are tossed on this open sea; we, the storm-tossed, entreat you to come to our aid, most holy [Virgin], outstanding star of the sea, you who for this are appointed merciful, just as you bring protection.

Nothing which you have prayed for, [Virgin] singular in piety, has your very own Son denied you: your offspring, by your entreaty, gets rid of the horrible refuse of sinners from those who love you.

How, then, can we be empty of thy praises, holy mother. Hear us, and those who have been taken out of sin, the lovers of your Son; prepare them to enjoy blessed light in the palace of heaven. Amen.

Comment: None.

12. *Hac clara die turma,* ff. 190_v-191.

Text: Analecta Hymnica, VII, No. 101 and LIII, No. 98; Milchsack, No. 244.

- v - v- v -|

Scansion: Hac clara die turma

v -v -

festiva dat

v -v-

preconia

Type: classical.

Translation: On this bright day a happy troop is offering public praises to Mary by striking up symphonious sounds sweet as nectar. You alone, [Mary,] are the mistress of the world, the most pure, the queen of virgins, the cause of salvation, the door of life, and you are filled with the grace of heaven.

For angelic messages were once made to her: "Hail, Mary, full of grace forever; within the holy ranks of women [thou art] always blessed, a virgin and pregnant mother, chaste, with glorious offspring."

To which Mary returned these words: "[How have your messages been made to me!] I have certainly had no sexual relations with young men. And how have I given birth unimpaired." The messenger then replied with this divine address: "Thou art filled with sacred breath, Mary, bearing new joys from heaven to earth, by the introduction of a Son. You bear, closed within thy womb, Him who rules forever, and Him who at all times makes peace."

Comment: Probably the oldest text in the W_1 collection, this sequence makes use of the assonant "a" typical of the St. Martial school, and was in existence in the repertoire of that institution as early as 935 A. D. (in monophonic guise).[61] A curiosity occurs in the second

60 Supplied from *Analecta Hymnica,* VII, No. 101.

61 Ellinwood, "The Conductus," p. 189.

double versicle in W_1. In II, a, the usual words *virginum regina* (and corresponding notes) are omitted. In II, b, however, which is written in the margin, the words *referta gratia* (normally the paradigms of *virginum regina)* are included, but there are no notes for them. This error could indicatesome tampering with, or modification of the original, or it could simply be carelessness. The text of versicle V, b is omitted completely. Furthermore, Milchsack has arranged the versicles incorrectly from versicle VI on. For the correct arrangement see transcription No. 12.

13. *Virgo parens gaudeat,* ff. 191-191v.

Text: Analecta Hymnica, VIII, No. 81; Milchsack, No. 245.

- v - v - v- |
Scansion: Virgo parens gaudeat
- v - v - - |
Virgo semper pura
- v - v - v - |
Parens sine corporis
- v - v - -
Et mentis laesura.

Type: mature (7/6/7/6).

Translation: May the obedient Virgin rejoice, the Virgin ever pure, the parent without injury of body and mind; unheard of novelty, a new begetting, which knows not the frail laws of procreation.

A rod, symbolic of the Virgin, prepares a flower without root; [similarly] a virgin prepares the Saviour without seed. A bush in flame does not experience heat; [similarly] a mother does not lose her chastity in childbirth. The gate of the Lord is revealed to no man; [similarly] the birth is made inaccessible forever, the fountain is sealed.

The root of Jesse shoots forth, is fruitful with flower, and is enriched sevenfold by the gift of the spirits. The morning star rises in the evening, light is created in darkness, salvation in disaster. Medicine drops on sick beings; the Lord visited disasters with medicine.

The Father sent a messenger, the messenger is heard. A virgin trusts, a deity is co-united with flesh. A mother is impregnated, the father knows her not; without the mother of the Son, the Father is discovered. The substance is triple, the nature is double, unity of person is wonderfully conjoined. They are separate in every way, creator and offspring, of which the measuring, consider, falls under number.

Virgin Mary, obtain grace for us; intercede with thy Son, holy mediator, lest, while the way of God's mandate is being run, fantasy should run between our steps. Amen.

Comment: The meter is quite consistent throughout, but there appears to be an occasional shift to iambic, and frequently the penultimate syllable is stretched to cover a whole foot, which in turn creates lines equivalent to eight and seven syllables instead of seven and six, that is, this sequence also shows signs of "regularization." Its acceptance in W_1 would appear to predate any of the sources listed in Analecta Hymnica.

14. *Verbum bonum et suave,* ff. 191_v-192.

Text: Analecta Hymnica, LIV, No. 218; Kehrein, No. 268; Milchsack, No. 246.

```
                   - v   - v| -  v- v|
Scansion:  Verbum bonum et suave
                   - v - v|- v  -v|
           Personemus illud ave
                   -   v     -v -  v  -v|
           Per quod Christi fit conclave
                   - v  - v  -v-
           Virgo mater filia;
```

Type: regular (8/8/8/7).

Translation: Let us resound the good sweet word, that *Ave* by which the virgin mother of Christ is made a filial room; greeted by that *Ave,* the fruitful Virgin, born of the line of David, a lily amongst thorns, soon conceived.

Hail! mother of Solomon's truth, fleece of Gideon, whose childbearing the wise men praise with three gifts. Hail! You have created the sun! Hail! You have brought forth fruit! You have conferred life and authority on a slipping world!

Hail! mother of the highest word, port of the sea, sign of the thornbush, rod of vapour, leader of the fragrant angels, we humbly beseech that you improve us, that you commend our improvement to your son, so that we might have eternal joy. Amen.

Comment: none.

EDITORIAL NOTE

As explained above, the sequences which follow have been transcribed according to the principle that syllabic grouping, defined by *Silbenstriche,* is associated with poetic meter which in turn is directly related to musical meter. The rhythm of regular and mature sequences presents few problems because of consistent patterning, but such is not the case with those that are irregular. In the latter, syllables are also clearly grouped but in an irregular fashion. It is the belief of the present writer that the rhythm of the latter has been reduced to a mixture of iambs and trochees, and can also be retrieved according to grouping, and the positioning of groups. Accordingly, groups of six syllables usually indicate iambic meter, groups of seven, trochaic, and groups of four and eight at the beginning of a versicle would indicate trochaic meter if followed by an odd-numbered group; groups of two and three syllables are determined by their context.

The transcriptions have been rendered in $^{6}/_{4}$ time, but in the irregular sequences barring does not always work out evenly; final measures sometimes contain only two or three beats instead of six, and rather than adjusting these measures to the artificially imposed barring (by change of time signature or the addition of rests) they have been left incomplete. Also, rests at the ends of versicles are sometimes required on the first sounding of a versicle but not on the second, or vice versa, owing to shifts of meter; such rests have been put into parentheses in the transcriptions. Ligatures have been indicated in the standard way by horizontal brackets; since the numerous descending *currentes* have been considered an alternate form of writing ligatures, they too have been so indicated. In the manuscript, plicas appear in two ways, either alone or in conjunction with another note (and respectively); the distinction has been preserved in the transcriptions (and). *Silbenstriche* have been indicated above the transcriptions by apostrophes, quilismata by a saw-toothed symbol ( ), and *musica ficta* has been approached in roughly the same manner as adopted by Waite,[62] that is, only those flat signs that appear in the manuscript have been introduced, except for instances when a flattened note appears directly above or below a note of the same pitch (e. g., see No. 4, versicle III). Sometimes notes in the manuscript are inordinately elongated (e. g., ,); occasionally they would seem to require lengthening in transcription, especially at cadences. All fermatas are editorial. The spelling in the texts has been brought into line with standard dictionary form, with contradictions (such as "e" for "ae") and abbreviations written out in full.

Other problems and emendations of an editorial nature are listed below with the appropriate sequences referred to by number. Editorial problems and/or alterations are indicated by versicle numbers and the measure(s) therein (e. g., V, 3); where textual difficulties occur the reference will be further qualified by a letter (e. g., V,b,3). Since the Milchsack version of the texts is the only complete edition in existence, and since there are a number of errors in that version, the disparities between the texts in this edition and those in the former will be pointed out. If a sequence is not listed below, then no editorial changes were made: [62]

1. VI,b,3—text is obscured, nor could Milchsack decipher it, but the word, according to meaning, appearance, and metrical context, would seem to be *misericordiam.*

VI,b,5-6—Milchsack reads *faciens.*

VI,8—*Silbenstrich* missing in MS.

2. I,1—the meter is unclear because of the unusual grouping (4/6/7/3) of the versicle, but has been interpreted as *fractio modi.*

IV,a,4—Milchsack reads *utero.*

IV,b,5—*quod* omitted in Milchsack.

VI,a,4—Milchsack reads *respirant.*

VI,1—the melisma on "O" is unusual, but since the tenor constitutes a group of seven notes, the meter has been interpreted as trochaic.

3. IX,1—Milchsack reads *Ut.*

4. IV,a,1—Milchsack and the MS read *ortus,* but *hortus* makes much better sense

5. III,a,3—Milchsack reads *carnis.*

IV,b,1—Milchsack reads *virgo.*

VII,1—the melisma on "O" breaks the normal patterning, but as in some final *Amen*s, groups of three notes in the tenor have been interpreted as covering the whole foot.

VIII,b,4—Milchsack reads *flebili.*

6. III,b to IV,b—The order of versicles is incorrect in Milchsack.

IV,2—*Silbenstrich* omitted in MS.

V,a,3-5—Milchsack reads *Mariae* instead of *Gabrieli* which robs the versicle of a syllable. He also adds the word *veraci,* which, along with

62 Waite, *opere citato.,* p. 137.

Mariae, does not appear in the MS.

V,b,4—Milchsack reads *Maria.*

7. II,a,4—Milchsack reads *dignam.*

II,b,5—the "ia" is missing in MS; Milchsack reads *Mariam.*

III,a and b—at this point, Milchsack incorrectly divides the sequence into two further sequences, thus giving the impression that there are three separate numbers instead of one. The ordering of the stanzas is also incorrect in Milchsack.

IV,a,1-2—*fractio modi* (this does not occur on the repeat).

VII,b,8—Milchsack reads *sit.*

VIII,b,end—Milchsack incorrectly places the final *Amen.*

10. II,3—Milchsack reads *visu.*

VII,4—the symbol "*p*" has been interpreted as an indication of the portion of music to be used for the final unnotated *Amen.*

12. II,b,end—the words *referta gratia* appear in the MS but there is no music for them. This suggests that this relatively aged sequence had been modified.

V,b—text of whole versicle omitted in MS. The missing line has been supplied from *Analecta Hymnica* VII, No. 101. Milchsack has omitted it.

VI,b to VII,b—order of the versicles is incorrect in Milchsack.

13. I,b,5—Milchsack reads *que.*

II,b,1—Milchsack reads *Rubes.*

II,b,7—Milchsack reads *non.*

III,b,5—Milchsack reads *septem qui.*

IV,a,5—Milchsack reads *sit.*

1. Mittit ad virginem

IV
a) Ac - ce-de nun - ti - a dic a - ve com - mi - nus dic ple-na gra - ti - a
b) Vir - go sus - ci - pi - as De - i de-po - si - tum in quo per - fi - ci - as
dic te - cum do - mi - nus et dic ne ti - me - as;
cas - ta pro - po - si - tum et vo - tum te - ne - at;
V
a) A - u - dit et
b) Con - si - li - a -
sus - ci - pit pu - el - la nun - ti - um cre - dit et con - ci - pit et pa - rit fi -
ri - um hu - ma - ni ge - ne - ris et De - um for - ti - li et pa - trem pos -
li - um sed ad - mi - ra - bi - le
te - ris in pa - ce sta - bi - lem.
VI
a) Qui no - bis tri - bu - at
b) Re - is im - per - ti - ens
pec - ca - ti ve - ni - am re - a - tus di - lu - at et do - nec pa - tri - am
mi - se - ri - cor - di - am ser - vos - que fa - ti - ens per ma - tris gra - ti - am
in ar - ce - si - de - rum;
con - sor - tes su - pe - rum.
A - - - men.

2. Paranimphus salutat virginem

3. Ave Maria gratia plena

ti pa-cem ho-mi-ni-bus et an-ge-lis glo-ri-am;
des ut es-se-mus su-i nos fe-cit per gra-ti-am.
IV
a) Per hoc au-tem a-ve mun-do tam su-a-ve con-tra car-nis iu-
b) Ge-nu-is-ti pro-lem no-vum stel-la so-lem no-va ge-ni-tu-
ra;
ra.
V
a) Tu par-vi et mag-ni le-o-nis et ag-ni sal-
b) Tu flo-ris et ro-ris pa-nis et pas-to-ris vir-
va-to-ris Chris-ti tem-plum ex-ti-tis-ti sed vir-go in-tac-ta;
gi-num re-gi-na ro-sa si-ne spi-na ge-ne-trix es fac-ta.
VI
a) Tu ci-vi-tas re-gis ius-ti-ti-ae;
b) Tu ma-ter es mi-se-ri-cor-di-ae.
VII
a) De la-cu fae-cis et mi-se-ri-ae;
b) The-o-phi-lum re-for-mans gra-ti-ae.
VIII
a) Er-go ma-ris stel-la ver-bi De-
b) Pa-ra-di-si por-ta per quam lux

4. Hodiernae lux diei

III
IV
V
ci - ni - a;
gra - ti - a.
a) A - ve do - mi - na cae-lo - rum in - ex-per - ta
b) Fe - cun - da - ta si - ne vi - ro ge - nu-is - ti
vi - ri tho - rum pa - rens pa - ris nes - ci - a;
mo - do mi - ro ge - ni - to - rem fi - li - a.
a) Flo - rens hor - tus aus - tro flan - te por - ta clau - sa post et an - te
b) Fu - sa cae - li ro - re tel - lus fu - sum Ge - de - o - nis vel - lus
vi - a vi - ris in - vi - a;
de - i - ta - tis plu - vi - a.
a) Sal - ve splen - dor fir - ma - men - ti tu ca - li - gi - no - sae men - ti de - su - per ir - ra - di - a;
b) Pla - ca ma - re ma - ris stel - la ne in - vol - vat nos pro - cel - la et tem - pes - tas ob - vi - a.
A - - - - - men.

5. Ave, mundi spes, Maria

VII
VIII
IX
X
est vir - gi - ni - tas; a)O quam dig - na, quam se - re - na,
sit fe - cun - di - tas. b)A qua ser - vi - tus fi - ni - tur
quam be - nig - na, quam a - moe - na, ex qua Chris - tus nas - ci - tur;
por - ta cae - li a - pe - ri - tur et li - ber - tas red - di - tur.
a) O cas - ti - ta - tis li - li - um tu - um pre - ca - re
b) Ne nos pro nos - tro vi - ti - o in dis - tric - to iu -
fi - li - um qui sa - lus est hu - mi - li - um;
di - ci - o sub - ji - ci - at sup - pli - ci - o.
Sed nos tu - a sanc -
ta pre - ce mun - dans a pec - ca - ti fae - ce Col - lo - cet in lu -
cis do - mo; a - men di - cat om - nis ho - - mo.

6. Virgini Mariae laudes

7. Laudes Christo decantemus

V
er - pe - ra; a)Haec est sca-la pec - ca - to - rum per quam Chris-tus rex cae - lo - rum
la - mi - ne. b)For-ma cu - ius sin - gu - la - ris per quam ro - ris sa - lu - ta - ris
VI
des - cen - dit ad in - fi - ma; a)Is - ta su - os for - ti - o - res
do - na dan - tur in - ti - ma. b)Dat cap - ti - vis li - ber - ta - tem
sem - per fa - cit et vic - to - res ae - gros sa - nat et lan - guo - res
vi - tae con - fert no - vi - ta - tem ad an - ti - quam dig - ni - ta - tem
VII
re - pri - mit dae - mo - ni - a; a)Vir - go sig - num spe - ci - a - le
haec re - du - xit om - ni - a. b)Me - di - ci - na Chris - ti - a - na
mun - di ve - ra sa - lus va - le in - ter sig - na nul - lum ta - le
sal - va sa - nos ae - gros sa - na quod non va - let vis hu - ma - na
VIII
fron - de flo - re ger - mi - ne; a)As - sis - ten - tes ma - tris lau - di
fit in tu - o no - mi - ne. b)Ut quos ma - tri vis ser - vi - re

8. Missus Gabriel de caelis

ca - ro fac - tum sem - per ta - men est in - tac - tum pu - el - la - re
non de - flo - rat non tor - que - tur nec la - bo - rat quan - do pa - rit
III
gre - mi - um; a) Sig - num au - dis no - vi - ta - tis cre - de so - lum
fi - li - um. b) Sig - num gran-de et in - sig - ne est in ru - bo
et est sa - tis non est tu - ae fa - cul - ta - tis sol - ve - re cor -
et in ig - ne nec ad - pro - pi - et in - dig - ne cal - ce - a - tus
IV
ri - gi - am; a) Vir - ga sic - ca si - ne ro - re no - vo ri - tu
quis - pi - am. b) Be - ne - dic - tus ta - lis fruc - tus fruc-tus gau - di -
no - vo mo - re fruc - tum pro - tu - lit cum flo - re sic et vir - go
i non luc - tus non e - rit A - dam se - duc - tus si de hoc gus -
V
pe - pe-rit; a) Je - sus nos - ter Je - sus bo - nus pi - ae ma - tris pi - um o - nus
ta - ve-rit. b) Qui sic est pro no - bis na - tus nos-tros de - le - at re - a - tus

9. *Virgo mitis verae vitis*

10. Reginarum dominam

11. *Ave, caeli imperatrix*

12. Hac clara die turma

IV
ge - li - ca: a) Mu - li - e - rum pi - a ag - mi - na in - tra sem -
sae - cu - la. b) Vir - go et gra - vi - da ma - ter in - tac - ta pro -
per be - ne - dic - ta,
le glo - ri - o - sa.
V
a) Cu - i con - tra Ma - ri - a haec
[b) In me quo - mo - do tu - a iam
red - dit fa - mi - na:
fi - ent nun - ti - a?]
VI
a) Vi - ri no - vi nul - lam cer - te
b) Ex quo at - que na - ta sum in -
co - pu - lam,
cor - rup - ta.
VII
a) Di - va mis-sus i - ta red - dit af - fa - ta:
b) Fla - tu sa - cro ple - na fi - es, Ma - ri - a,
VIII
a) No - va ef - fe - rens gau - di - a cae - lo ter - rae na - ti per ex -
b) In - tra tu - i u - te - ri claus-tra por - tas qui gu - ber - nat
or - di - a,
ae - ter - na.
IX
Om - ni - a qui et tem - po - ra pa - ci - fi - cat.

13. *Virgo parens gaudeat*

IV
na - tur; a)O - ri - tur in ves - pe - re stel - la ma - tu - ti - na, lu - men fit in te - ne-bris sa - lus in ru - i - na;
ta - tur. b)Ae - gris a - ni - man - ti - bus stil - lat me - di - ci - na, vi - si - ta - vit Do - mi - nus ma - la me - di - ci - na.
V
a) Pa - ter mi - sit nun - ti - um nun - ti - us au - di - tur, vir - go cre - dit de - i - tas, car - ni co - u - ni - tur;
b) Im - preg - na - tur ge - ni - trix ge - ni - tor nes - ci - tur, si - ne ma - tre fi - li - i, pa - ter in - ve - ni - tur.
VI
a)Trip - lex est sub - stan - ti - a ge - mi - na na - tu - ra, per - so - na - lis u - ni - tas mi - ra con - ivnc - tu - ra;
b)Dis - tant in hu - ius - mo - di fac - tor et fac - tu - ra, quae ca - dit sub nu - me - ro pon - de - ris men - su - ra.

14. Verbum bonum et suave

II
a) A - ve ve - ri Sa - lo - mo - nis ma - ter vel - lus Ge - de - o - nis
b) A - ve so - lem ge - nu - is - ti a - ve pro - lem pro - tu - lis - ti
cu - ius ma - gi tri - bus do - nis lau - dant pu - er - pe - ri - um;
mun - do lap - so con - tu - lis - ti vi - tam et im - pe - ri - um.
III
a) A - ve ma - ter ver - bi sum - mi ma - ris por - tus sig - num du - mi
b) Sup - pli - ca - mus nos e - men - da e - men - da - tos nos com - men - da
a - ro - ma - tum vir - ga fu - mi an - ge - lo - rum do - mi - na;
tu - o na - to ad ha - ben - da sem - pi - ter - na gau - di - a.
A - - - - - - - - - - - - - - men.

SELECTED BIBLIOGRAPHY

Anderson, Gordon A. *The Latin Compositions in Fascicules VII and VIII of the Notre Dame Manuscript Wolfenb⁵ttel 1099 (1206).* (Musicological Studies/Wissenschaftliche Abhandlungen, 24.) Brooklyn, N. Y.; The Institute of Mediaeval Music, 1968.

Anderson, Gordon A. "The Rhythm of *cum littera* Sections of Polyphonic Conductus in Mensural Sources," *The Journal of the American Musicological Society,* XXVI (1973), 288-304.

Anderson, Gordon A. "Symbolism in Texts of Thirteenth-Century Music," *Studies in Music,* IV (1970), 19-59.

Anderson, Gordon A. "Thirteenth-Century Conductus: *Obiter Dicta,"The Musical Quarterly,* LVIII (1972), 349-364.

Anthon, Charles. *A System of Latin Prosody and Metre.* New York: Harper and Bros., 1860.

Anglès, Higini. "Eine Sequenzensammlung mit Mensuralnotation und volkstümlichen Melodien," in *Speculum Musicae Artis.* München:- Wilhelm Fink Verlag, 1970. (Pages 9-18.)

Apel, Willi. *The Notation of Polyphonic Music 900-1600.* Cambridge, Mass.: The Mediaeval Academy of America, 1953.

Bartsch, Karl. *Die lateinischen Sequenzen des Mittelalters.* Hildesheim: Georg Olms, 1968. (This is a reprint of the 1868 edition.)

Baxter, J. H. *An Old St. Andrews Music Book.* London: Humphrey Milford for the Oxford University Press, 1950.

Beare, William. *Latin Verse and European Song.* London: Methuen and Co., 1957.

Bent, Ian. "A New Polyphonic Verbum Bonum et Suave," *Music and Letters,* LI (1970), 227-241.

Benton, John F. "Nicolas of Clairvaux and the Twelfth-Century Sequence," *Traditio,* XVIII (1962), 149-179.

Chevalier, Ulysse. *Repertorium Hymnologicum.* 6 vols. Louvain/Leuven: Imprimerie Lefever, 1892-1920.

Coussemaker, Edmund de. *Scriptorum de Musica Medii Aevi.* 4 vols. Paris: A Durand, 1864.

Dittmer, Luther A. *Firenze Biblioteca Mediceo-Laurenziana, Pluteo 29,1.* 2 vols (Publications of Mediaeval Musical Manuscripts/Veröffentlichungen mittelalterlicher Musikhandschriften Nos. 10 and 11.) Brooklyn, N. Y.: The Institute of Mediaeval Music, 1968 and 1971.

Dittmer, Luther A. *Madrid 20486.* (Publications of Mediaeval Musical Manuscripts/Veröffentlichungen mittelalterlicher Musikhandschriften No. 1.) Brooklyn, N. Y.: The Institute of Mediaeval Music, 1958.

Dittmer, Luther A. *Wolfenbuttel 1099.* (Publications of Mediaeval Musical Manuscripts/Veröffentlichungen mittelalterlicher Musikhandschriften No. 2 (Brooklyn, N. Y.: The Institute of Mediaeval Music, 1960.

Dreves, G. M., in collaboration with C. Blume and M. Bannister. *Analecta Hymnica.* 55 vols. Leipzig: O. R. Reisland, 1886-1922.

Dronke, Peter. *The Medieval Lyric.* London: Hutchinson versity Library, 1968.

Faral, EM *Les Arts Poetiques du XIIe et du XIIIe Siècle.* (Bibliothèque de l'Ecole des Hautes Etudes, No. 238.) Paris: Librairie Ancienne Honoré Champion, 1924.

Faral, E. *Les Arts Poétiques du XIIe et du XIIIe Siècle.* (Bibliothèque de l'Ecole des Hautes Etudes, No. 238.) Paris: Librairie Ancienne Honoré Champion, 1924.

Flotzinger, Rudolf, *Der Diskantussatz im Magnus Liber und seine Nachfolge.* (Wiener musikwissenschaftliche Beiträge, Band 8) Wien: Hermann Bohlaus Nachf., 1969.

Gallo, Ernest, *The Poetria Nova and its Sources in Early Rhetorical Doctrine.* Paris: Mouton, 1971.

Gerbert, Martin. *Scriptores Ecclesiastici de Musica.* 3 vols. Milano: Bollettino Bibliografico Musicale, 1931. (Reprint of the 1784 edition.)

Gillingham, Bryan R. *A History of the Polyphonic Sequence in the Middle Ages.* Ph. D. dissertation. University of Washington, 1976. (Microfilm. Ann Arbor: University Microfilms.)

Gillingham, Bryan R. "Modal Rhythm and the Medieval Sequence," *Studies in Music at the University of Western Ontario,* I (1976), 105-123.

Handschin, Jacques. "A Monument of English Mediaeval Polyphony," *The Musical Times,* LXXIII (1932), 510-513 and LXXIV (1933), 697-704.

Handschin, Jacques. "Trope, Sequence, and Conductus," in *The New Oxford History of Music.* Edited by Dom Anselm Hughes. London: Oxford University Press, 1955. (Pages 128-174.)

Haskins, C. H. *The Renaissance of the Twelfth Century.* Cambridge, Mass.: Harvard University Press, 1927.

Kehrein, Josef. *Lateinische Sequenzen des Mittelalters.* Mainz: F. Kupferberg, 1944.

Ludwig, Friedrich. *Repertorium Organorum Recentioris et Motetorum Vetustissimi Stili.* 2 vols. in 3. Brooklyn, N. Y.: The Institute of Mediaeval Music, 1964, 1971, and 1978. (Vol. I,1 first appeared in 1910.)

Migne, J. P. *Patrologia Cursus Completus. Series Latina.* 221 vols. Tournholti, Belgium: Typographi Brepols Editores Pontificii, 1844-1864.

Milchsack, Gustav. *Hymni et Sepuentiae cum pluribus aliis et Latinis et Gallicis necnon Theotuscis Carminibus medio aevo compositis.* Halle a_S: Maximiliani Niemeyer, 1886.

Misset, E., et P. Aubry. *Les Proses d'Adam de St-Victor.* Paris: H.

Welter, 1900.

Rary, F. J. E. *A History of Christian Latin Poetry.* Oxford: Clarendon Press, 1927.

Répertoire International des Sources Musicales. A continuing series, with various editors and publishers, sponsored by the International Musicological Society and the International Association of Music Libraries.

Roesner, Edward M. "The Origins of W_1," *The Journal of the American Musicological Society,* XXIX (1976), 337-380.

Rohloff, Ernest. *Die Quellenhandschriften zum Musiktraktat des Johannes de Grocheo.* Leipzig: VEB deutscher Verlag für Musik, 1967.

Sanders, E. H. "Peripheral Polyphony of the Thirteenth Century," *The Journal of the American Musicological Society,* XV (1962), 250-291.

Szövérffy, Josef. *Die Annalen der lateinischen Hymnendichtung.* 2 vols. Berlin: Erich Schmidt Verlag, 1964.

Taliaferro, R. C. *St. Augustine on Music.* Annapolis: The St. John's Bookstore, 1939.

Waesberghe, J. Smits van. *Expositiones in Micrologum Guidonis Aretini.* Amsterdam, 1957.

Waite, William. *The Rhythm of Twelfth-Century Polyphony.* New Haven: Yale University Press, 1954.

INDEX